Don't Leave Hungry

Don't Leave Hungry

Fifty Years of Southern Poetry Review

Edited by James Smith

Foreword by Billy Collins

The University of Arkansas Press
Fayetteville
2009

ISBN-10 (cloth): 1-55728-892-5
ISBN-13 (cloth): 978-1-55728-892-9

ISBN-10 (paper): 1-55728-893-3
ISBN-13 (paper): 978-1-55728-893-6

12   11   10   09   08   5   4   3   2   1

Text design by Ellen Beeler

⊗ The paper used in this publication meets the minimum requirements of the
American National Standard for Permanence of Paper for Printed Library Materials
Z39.48-1984.

Library of Congress Cataloging-in-Publication Data

Don't leave hungry : Fifty years of Southern poetry review / edited by
  James Smith ; foreword by Billy Collins.
       p. cm.
  Includes bibliographical references and index.
  ISBN-13: 978-1-55728-892-9 (alk. paper)
  ISBN-10: 1-55728-892-5 (alk. paper)
  ISBN-13: 978-1-55728-893-6 (pbk. : alk. paper)
  ISBN-10: 1-55728-893-3 (pbk. : alk. paper)
  1. American poetry—20th century. 2. American poetry—21st century.
  I. Smith, James, 1962– II. Southern poetry review.
  PS615.D645 2009
  811'.5408—dc22
                                                                    2008036499

Acknowledgments

Grateful acknowledgment is made to all of the poets and executors who graciously allowed *Southern Poetry Review* to reprint poems from earlier issues. Those who requested a credit line are noted below.

Some poems appear as revised versions, changed usually in minor ways, according to the writers' wishes. Most of the poems, however, appear as they did originally in the pages of the journal.

I am grateful for the inestimable help of Enid Shomer and Lawrence J. Malley at the University of Arkansas Press. Many thanks to Robert Parham, the editor of *Southern Poetry Review,* for the opportunity to edit the anthology. Fred Courtright at The Permissions Company guided me through all questions about permission. Stephanie Roberts, the journal's editorial assistant, proved invaluable month after month. Armstrong Atlantic State University awarded me a summer grant in 2006 for focused work on the project. Finally, the patience and encouragement of family and friends made it possible to keep what turned out to be this often-overwhelming commitment. I am particularly grateful to my parents and Andrew Hasbrouck.

Suzanne Cleary. "Anyways" from *Trick Pear.* Copyright © 2007 by Suzanne Cleary. Reprinted by permission of Carnegie Mellon University Press.

Judith Ortiz Cofer. "La Tristeza" from *Reaching for the Mainland and Selected New Poems.* Copyright © 1995 by Bilingual Press/Editorial Bilingue, Arizona State University (Tempe). Reprinted by permission of the publisher.

James Dickey. "The Falls." Copyright © 2009 by Christopher Dickey, Kevin Dickey and Bronwen Dickey. Reprinted with permission of McIntosh & Otis, Inc.

Jean Farley. "Language of Flowers" from *Figure and Field.* Copyright © 1970 by the University of North Carolina Press. Reprinted by permission of the publisher.

David Ignatow. "My poetry is for the night" from *New and Collected Poems.* Copyright © 1986 by David Ignatow. Reprinted by permission of Wesleyan University Press. "The book flies open" reprinted by permission of Yaedi Ignatow.

Carolyn Kizer. "How It Passes" from *Yin.* Copyright © 1984 by Carolyn Kizer. Reprinted by permission of BOA Editions, Ltd., www.boaeditions.org.

Denise Levertov. "Heights, Depths, Silence, Unceasing Sound of the Surf" from *Poems, 1972–1982.* Copyright © 1982 by Denise Levertov. Reprinted by permission of New Directions Publishing Corp.

Jim Wayne Miller. "How America Came to the Mountains" from *The Brier Poems.* Reprinted by permission of Gnomon Press.

Vassar Miller. "Lady of Leisure" from *Onions and Roses.* Copyright © 1968 by Vassar Miller. Reprinted by permission of Wesleyan University Press.

Judson Mitcham. "Loss of Power" from *A Little Salvation: Poems Old and New.* Copyright © 2007 by Judson Mitcham. Reprinted by permission of the University of Georgia Press.

Robert Morgan. "Plankroad" from *Groundwork*. Reprinted by permission of Gnomon Press.

Sharon Olds. "The Domesticators" from *Southern Poetry Review* (Fall 1977). Reprinted by permission of the poet.

William Stafford. "Mother Talking in the Porch Swing" from *Southern Poetry Review* (Fall 1975). Reprinted by permission of the Estate of William Stafford.

Contents

Chapter 2: The 1970s   39

Chapter 3: The 1980s   103

Chapter 4: The 1990s   169

Chapter 5: The 2000s   245

Foreword

To be honest, I had never heard of *Southern Poetry Review* before I submitted some of my poems to them in the 1970s. Such a confession says nothing about the reputation of the journal but rather speaks of my ignorance of the literary marketplace at the time, as well as my then-shameless hunger to be published. Like some other writers who have only recently summoned the hopefulness required to toss their writing into the public eye, I had fallen into the unfortunate habit of reading literary magazines with one thing in mind—how to get into them. Instead of reading the essays for insights, the fiction for narrative journeys, and the poetry for imaginative thrills, I was looking only for cracks in the editorial wall that would allow me to slip into the ranks of the Published and forever leave the hoard of the Anonymous. I had a plan: first, to be noticed by a magazine's readership, then the literary community at large and shortly thereafter, the world itself. So fuzzy was my mental picture of the literary marketplace, I would send out poems scatter-gun fashion and hope for the best—not a winning strategy as one rejection slip after another would remind me. When *Southern Poetry Review* joined that very select group of magazines willing to accept a poem or two of mine, I was probably guilty of mistaking luck for destiny. I remember thinking that the magazine's name had a solid regional ring to it, but I confess I would have been equally thrilled had my work been accepted by the Eastern, Northern, or Western Poetry Reviews, if such publications had existed.

Today, I am a slightly wiser man who recognizes *Southern Poetry Review* as one of the nation's pre-eminent literary magazines and, by American standards, a veteran publication. Founded by poet Guy Owen in 1958 and edited by him until 1977, the magazine has moved its home base from Florida to North Carolina and now finds itself based at Armstrong Atlantic State University in Savannah, Georgia, thus preserving its regional name.

But *Southern Poetry Review* was never a review of only "southern poetry," about which I will say only that I know it when I read it. Lines like "He was just a little feller" and the speculation that God's name might be "Bubba" remind me quickly where we are. The same goes for poems about okra (or is it "okry?"), as well as reflections on the Civil War—a rare subject in "northern poetry." Extrapolating the standards of the editors from the poetry collected here, it would seem that a poem containing kudzu or catfish was not rejected by reason of its possibly limited down-home appeal. Nor was the magazine's doorway narrowed by a preference for a single poetic style. So wide is the editorial entrance that this golden-anniversary collection provides us with a generous overview of the various shapes American poetry has taken over the past half century. Even in the earliest issues, we find a very traditional poem of three *abab* quatrains next to a loose ramble by Howard Nemerov with unpredictable, interruptive line breaks.

Every year, thousands of poems come across the editorial desks of *Southern Poetry Review,* and the editors continue to follow Owen's publication philosophy—similar to that of Harriet Monroe's at *Poetry*—by printing a mix of established and fledgling voices. The present gathering of poems selected from fifty years' worth of issues contains poets who have become household names, at least in households where poetry is admitted, as well as lesser-known authors. One interesting aspect of the anthology is the opportunity to see examples of the early styles of some poets with whom we are all familiar. We catch some of them early on in their poetic development before they have settled into their distinctive manner. James Dickey produces this curiously strained metaphor: "To look purely into the sky, / As the current possesses my body / Like a wind, and blows through / Land I have walked on." We also see David Kirby before he found either his shifting, story-telling style or his ragged-edged stanza. Nor has Charles Wright in the early '70s arrived at his expansive, wandering voice; instead he is writing short imagistic poems with a haiku-like focus. And Albert Goldbarth offers an uncharacteristically laconic poem tidily shaped into tercets.

Other poets, in their early appearances, have already found the voice that will echo through their later poems. X. J. Kennedy could have written these smartly rhyming lines only yesterday:

> At Mount Rushmore I looked up into one
> Of those faces born joined to the same neck bone.
> I said, *Abe, Abe, how does it feel to be up there?*—
> And that great rock he has for a pupil budged, I swear,
> And he looked me right in the eye and he said, *Alone.*

William Matthews in the 1950s has developed the kind of vatic irony readers associate with his work, as well as the art of the line break:

> People are history
> but their belongings stay
> around. . . .
>
> The whole attic stinks
> of permanence.

Sharon Olds writes characteristically and disturbingly of a mother dying and leaving nothing but "dark pairs of shoes like the halves of shells." And it should come as no surprise that Stephen Dunn thirty-five years ago sounds like Stephen Dunn today, only not quite so sure in his wisdom. David Ignatow is represented by poems as beautifully mysterious as any he ever wrote, and Miller Williams knew early on how to amusingly overload a title: "How, Having Given Up the Classical Temper for the Romantic, We Try to Find Meaning in Death."

Bright gems are to be found in this commemorative anthology, among them the title poem of Henry Taylor's Pulitzer Prize–winning collection, *The Flying Change,* surely a sign of editorial prescience. Other stand-outs, for me, include Edward Wilson's moving "For the Woman in Her Station Wagon Weeping at a Red Light," Randolph Thomas's fanciful "Finishing the Puzzle," Bill Brown's disarming evocation of a near-death experience, and Lisa Erb Stewart's dark assessment of the physical self:

> Because
> the body thinks nothing—not even what day
> it is. Or its name. Or where it lies
>
> waiting to be touched by another body.
> The body doesn't care whose body.

And here is the twist of an ending to David R. Slavitt's poem on the shadowy appeal of Lamont Cranston:

> All of us know
> what evil lurks in the hearts of men. What's harder
> is what good and unremarkable
> except to the gazing eye, flawless, selfless
> as that glass, air, water. Obtuse, opaque,
> The Shadow got it wrong, knew nothing at all.

Also notable is Suzanne Cleary's "Anyways," a very funny and affecting poem about the delicate matter of correctness versus regional usage: "Anyone born anywhere near / my hometown says it this way, / with an *s* on the end: / 'The lake is cold, but I swim in it anyways,' / . . . We are shy, my people, not given to storytelling. / We end our stories too soon, trailing off 'Anyways . . .' / The carpenter sighs, 'I didn't need that finger anyways.' / The beauty school student sighs, 'It'll grow back anyways.'" And I was happy to find one of Philip Dacey's fine "New York Postcard Sonnets," this one on the New York Public Library's glorious Main Reading Room:

> Risen to glory, the high school study hall!
> Cellphone users here get their own circle in Hell.

As another sign of the magazine's diversity, the under-written exists side by side with the baroquely over-written. Compare sections of Lou Lipsitz:

> let's not
> say
> too much.

> let's
> keep
> the lines
> short.

to Kurt Leland's ode to poison ivy:

> Your trinity makes me think,

> spreading the month-long frissons of its anointing oils,
> that God is that spiritual discomfort whose
> blistering center is everywhere, the balm of whose
> circumference nowhere.

Appreciators of poetry's ability to compress will hearken to James Scruton's playful "The Names of Birds" (which ends with an echo of W. C. Fields: "my little widgeon, my chickadee"), as well as Robert West's pared-down, six-line elegy for Robert Creeley and Michelle Detorie's appropriately miniature "Doll House," which contains "a tiny rectangular / newspaper . . . a clock, / a fireplace, a crib."

Many of the inclusions encourage one to pay attention to the ways in which lyric poems move through a series of intensifying stages from a simple, everyday beginning to a revelatory, sometimes epiphanic ending. Greg Rappleye can advance in a mere twenty-eight lines from "I'd bring you cauliflower" to "binding the heart to silence." Robert Bense navigates his way from "I start with the car packed" to "I'm running from my life." And also finding a place here are a number of successfully restrained poems on dangerously charged subjects ranging from the first day of middle school to the oncologist's waiting room.

After I had completed my tour of the poems gathered here, I was reminded of a Lionel Trilling essay, "The Function of the Little Magazine," in which he decries the "great gulf between our educated class and the best of our literature." In the nineteenth century, Trilling contends, "literature was assumed"; it "underlay every activity of mind." But he points out that in his day—the essay was published in 1946—the place of literature had been co-opted by "the radio, movies, and certain magazines." How easy it would be to update the truth of his essay by adding iPods, DVDs, and the Internet—not to mention television itself—to his list of distractions. Hope, for Trilling, lies in the "little magazines"—are we not glad this diminutive epithet has gone out of style?—which have made a "heroic response" to the slackening of public interest in literature. No doubt, Trilling would have applauded the role of *Southern Poetry Review*, among others, in bringing to readers news of what is taking place on the front lines of contemporary poetry and poetic thought. This anniversary gathering of the best of the review provides a fine opportunity to weigh its significant contribution to our culture and to enjoy—without groaning—a groaning board of admirable poems.

Billy Collins

Introduction

Literary journals often keep the imprint of their founders all their lives, especially if those lives are short, as they tend to be, although *Southern Poetry Review* proves an exception there—fifty years old, and counting. When Guy Owen published *SPR*'s fifteenth-anniversary anthology with the University of North Carolina Press, in 1974, Louis D. Rubin Jr. praised the journal's superior quality in his introduction but also noted that "in not only surviving but flourishing for fifteen years, *SPR* has far eclipsed the national track record for most poetry magazines." Its longevity is especially remarkable because it publishes poetry only. In many journals, and certainly in major magazines that bother at all, as Owen notes, poems are "filler," not "the main course." *A Journal Dedicated to Poetry:* that's the logo the current editors gave *SPR,* and we like to think its founder would approve. For us, talking about Guy Owen is a way of talking about *Southern Poetry Review.*

The current editors think of it as Guy Owen's journal (not to diminish subsequent editors, including ourselves!) because his vision continues to sustain *SPR.* In his own time, he liked to say that the journal was "eclectic," looking for the best poetry it could find anywhere, on any topic, in any form. It maintains that quality to this day. Poet Betty Adcock, who worked on the editorial staff with Owen for eleven years, says that he wanted *SPR* to be "inclusive." Big names appeared beside names unknown, although the "unknowns" often became well-known enough. He was eager to find "emerging voices," says Adcock, especially young poets, noting that she was one of those encouraged early on by this passionate and persuasive editor.

He was a kind of Ezra Pound of the South (minus the overweening ego), an avid promoter of others: "The sole reason for little poetry journals such as ours," he wrote, "is to help poetry grow, to help the young poets along, until they can stand on their own." In taking this approach, Owen ultimately made *SPR* a "big" place of its own, one where established writers, as well, would want to appear. Too, because he felt that southern poets did not get a fair reading outside of the South, he made it clear that the journal was especially receptive to them, although it would never advocate what he called "a black-eyed peas and grits school of verse." More on that issue in a moment.

Owen began his journal in Deland, Florida, in 1958 as a small venue for the work of his creative writing students at Stetson College. He named it *Impetus*. "Great principle," notes second editor, Robert Grey, "but awful name." However, before the second issue came out, Owen's little project had attracted the notice of poets beyond Stetson, and he began to imagine a larger scope for it. He jokes that his students referred to the journal as "impotent," but it took several years and a move to North Carolina State University in Raleigh before he changed the name. When he did, however, he made it clear that although the title had changed, it was the same journal with the same goals. On the masthead of the first *Southern Poetry Review,* one finds the subheading, "formerly *Impetus*." With the name change, however, Owen raised the stakes and proved within a few years that his journal was anything but impotent.

The danger of what he called "a narrow provincialism" requires some assessment. Robert Grey felt that the name *Southern Poetry Review* hampered the journal, although he kept it when Owen passed *SPR* to him in 1978. By then, the name had stuck, for good and ill. "Some people assumed," Grey says, "we were racists and others assumed we were ignorant and provincial because of the term. Also, many writers, not just from the South, sent in stereotypical 'southern' poems which didn't do too much for anyone." According to Owen's longtime managing editor Mary C. Williams, "He wanted to foster Southern poetry and wanted *Southern* in the title of his magazine even though *SPR* was never regional in its acceptances." Adcock says that Owen envisioned an exceptional poetry journal that was "openly, proudly IN the South, but not only ABOUT the South." He made a risky move, but a brave and necessary one. The centers of literary arbitration might remain outside the South for some time, but Owen did not intend to give that power away willingly.

Owen is in agreement with Allen Tate when he quotes him: "The history of Southern poetry must constantly pause to enquire into the causes of our thin and not very comprehensive performance." But then Owen goes on to complain of the "brittle and dry quality" of some of the Fugitive poems, and although he just as readily decries the "substitution of raw energy for art and craftsmanship" that he finds in the Beat poets, he applauds them for getting poetry "out of the classrooms" and for their willingness "to take risks." He published poems from all over the country on a regular basis, as well as poems in translation from time to time, as all of *SPR*'s editors have done. Thus, he reminded southern readers to resist literary insularity. He was never a mindless booster for all things "southern." Owen wore many hats besides that of editor, and as a scholar of

American literature, not just southern literature, he demonstrated a keen sense of what his new journal might accomplish. Finally, anyone who took the time to open an issue could see plainly that Owen was not, as we say in the South, "just whistling 'Dixie.'"

Guy Owen was a successful teacher, scholar, editor, short story writer, and poet, as well as novelist. (In fact, all of *SPR*'s editors have been poets and teachers of literature.) Macmillan published his second novel, *The Ballad of the Flim-Flam Man,* in 1965, and George C. Scott starred in the successful film version. Owen co-wrote the screenplay. His third novel, *Journey for Joedel,* was published by Crown in 1970. It was nominated for the Pulitzer Prize. As a scholar, he received his doctorate at UNC–Chapel Hill in Renaissance literature. But most of his scholarly work centers on modern and contemporary American poetry. He edited and appeared in several collections of critical essays on American literature, and along with Mary C. Williams, he edited three anthologies of southern poetry. Williams and Adcock, among others, have stressed that Owen's passion was contemporary poetry. With such successful productivity in many other areas of literary endeavor, Owen's utter commitment to *SPR* is striking. Williams writes that when it came time, after twenty years, to pass his journal on, "he did not realize until afterwards that he had suffered an amputation."

Before that time came, however, Owen demonstrated generosity not only to poets who submitted work but also to those who helped him edit the journal. He might not have liked the fact that today we think of it as "Guy Owen's journal" because he included many others in the editorial process. For example, there always have been women editors at *SPR* (certainly not the norm in Owen's time), and he encouraged Adcock and Heather Ross Miller to edit a "women's issue" of the journal in the 1970s. He put an ad requesting submissions for this issue in the *New York Times Book Review,* and according to Adcock, poems poured in. In fact, she says, the submissions rate at *SPR,* in general, was tremendous. One of her keenest images of Owen's office: "grocery bags full of letters."

Another longtime editorial associate, Thomas N. Walters, writes of Owen's determination to overcome the severe adverse circumstances of his background, economic, environmental, hereditary. His demons motivated him to rise above them. To some extent, his generous, inclusive approach helped him to preserve himself. Adcock remembers his robust laugh and love of comic poems, his favorite expression "Splendid!" Williams remembers "Marvelous!" Both note that he wrote something on every rejection slip because he did not want to discourage.

Poet and fiction writer Robert Morgan reminds, however, that Owen balanced generosity with aesthetic discretion, noting "the unstinting generosity of his praise and the accuracy of his strictures." Owen published "The Falls," an early poem by the up-and-coming James Dickey, but he did not stint in his criticism of the poet's fourth book, *Helmets,* in a review several years later. After saying that Dickey's "arrogance" in his criticism also shows up in his latest poetry, Owen concludes: "James Dickey in his fourth volume is becoming diffuse and repetitious. He would do well to wait and take stock before risking another book soon." This example is important because Owen knew Dickey was and would be an important southern poet, and given his hopes for southern poetry, he would have wanted to promote Dickey, as he had in publishing him. However, he also wanted the poets of the region to grow, and whatever one's own thoughts about *Helmets* might be, Owen's convictions in that review are admirable. *SPR* practiced generosity, but not to the exclusion of discernment.

After Owen died at fifty-six, Adcock and Walters solicited funds—six thousand dollars—and in 1983 established the Guy Owen Prize, awarded annually since that time for a single, excellent poem. In 2008, when the journal turns fifty, the contest will celebrate its twenty-fifth anniversary: two significant milestones. Judged over the years by many of the best poets in contemporary poetry, this prize has been awarded to the "known" and the "unknown," to poets from all over the country, just as *SPR*'s founder would have wished. (See the appendix for the complete list of judges and winners.) At his death, Owen was not an obscure figure in American letters, nor was his journal. Among other places, his obituary ran in the *New York Times.*

Each editorial staff has brought something new to *SPR,* but they have all followed closely its founder's vision of it: eclectic, inclusive, encouraging. From 1978 to 1990, Robert Grey served as editor. From 1991 to 1993, Grey's wife, Lucinda, and Ken McLaurin, both former associate editors, worked as co-editors. Then, from 1994 to 2001, McLaurin led *SPR.* In 1978, when *SPR* moved from Raleigh's North Carolina State University to the University of North Carolina, in Charlotte, under Robert Grey, a column ran in the *Charlotte Observer* with this headline: "Poetry Review a Coup for City." By 2001, the journal was a North Carolina institution. In 2002, however, *SPR* moved to Savannah, Georgia, after its board chose Robert Parham to succeed Ken McLaurin. And the move made sense in many ways. Primarily, it was time for a change in the journal's format, and a move from its familiar home would allow more easily for the necessary reassessment.

When *SPR* came to Savannah, it had maintained its alternating single-color card-stock cover since 1978, and since Owen's time it had used all available space for poems. That is, if a second (or sometimes third) poem could fit on a single page, so be it. Give the reader as much poetry as possible, and no frills with the cover. It was an admirably pure and efficient plan, and as longtime readers of *SPR,* we were hesitant to tamper with it. It said, quietly, "What matters here is the poem. You are not going to get any flashy come-on from the cover." It was one of a few publications of its kind that still took this stance.

We consulted a lot of writers and editors, all of whom recommended change. The marketplace, they said, the marketplace! However, we knew that it should not be too drastic a change. Robert Parham and I opted for a cover design that would make use of black-and-white images. In photography and film, we reasoned, there is a kind of purist sensibility in black-and-white, so we felt we were staying true to the journal's past, in principle. If *SPR* had ever been "conservative," it was so in regard to its space. If a poem ended halfway down a page, the next poem would pick up not far below it. Years before the journal came to Savannah, however, I had heard poets complain about this treatment of their work. Most poets figure, "If it took a year, or more, to finish that poem, then it deserves its own space." I suggested that although we might print fewer poems, we would honor the work more by giving it breathing room. Too, the poet's name and the poem's title now would appear always at the top of their own page(s). It took a few years to refine the new look, inside and out, but with the arrival in 2004 of a new managing editor, Tony Morris, we found someone able to articulate the successful design we wanted.

One of the most fundamental issues that arose early on concerned our editorial role. Should we say to the poet whose work almost convinces us to publish it, "No, not this time, but try again with other poems"? Or should we initiate a conversation with the poet? Should we ask for revisions? We knew what this method would entail: a lot of correspondence back and forth about changes. Were we willing to commit to this sort of hands-on editorial process? As working poets, Parham and I valued most those editors who made suggestions about our work and regarded us as professional writers. It is the essence of the editorial enterprise to offer one's view when possible, bearing in mind always the limitations of one's own perspective, but nevertheless putting out there in plain sight one's guiding principles. However, once we put it into practice, I realized quickly the sort of labor this approach to editing required. But I am happy to report that our files contain many letters from poets praising our careful scrutiny and equally careful response to their poems. One of these won a Pushcart in 2005. We like to think that we continue Guy Owen's encouraging approach.

At *SPR,* we maintain the central tradition of two issues annually. We read between five thousand and seven thousand poems per year and publish approximately one hundred. It takes over four months to move from Day One (opening the first envelope from the slush pile) to Distribution. None of us gets paid a regular salary for editing the journal, although we receive some assistance from AASU, where the journal is housed. For anyone not familiar with this sort of endeavor, what might sound like a modest agenda (two issues/year) requires a staggering amount of work, especially from its three main editors, who also hold full-time jobs as academics. An independent, non-profit publication, the journal exists to publish poetry, not to make money, but it generates enough money through its contest and its submissions to allow us to publish two issues, advertise, and promote it at book fairs and conferences. It has received grants in the past, including from the NEA. In the early days, Owen and associates sometimes put up their own funds to keep his project alive. At times, it has had "patrons." We hope it will find them again. Since the 1970s it has maintained, on average, one thousand subscribers, many of them libraries that have carried the journal for decades. Its subscription base is national and international, as is its submissions base. Shelf sales are brisk. Most importantly, then, *Southern Poetry Review* is read.

Our anthology's title derives from a poem in it by Eleanor Ross Taylor, a southern poet undervalued for years. I was delighted to find "Don't Leave Hungry" as I read through *SPR*'s archives, selecting poems for this book. Not only is it strange and marvelous (that word again!) in its own right, but its commanding title has a "southern" ring to it that would satisfy Owen. Taylor's niece, Heather Ross Miller, also in the anthology and a former staff member, described Owen as "always encouraging us and welcoming us toward that table where so many crowd and so few get fed." Miller speaks of writers here and their desire for publication, but Owen also offered his journal as a table where he hoped readers would crowd and find plenty to feed them, no need to leave hungry.

James Smith
Savannah, Georgia

Works Cited

Adcock, Betty. Telephone interview. 17 March 2007.

Grey, Robert. Letter to Robert Parham. 16 January 2002.

Miller, Heather Ross. "Grand Guy Grand." *Pembroke Magazine* 13 (1981): 76–77.

Morgan, Robert. "Guy Owen as Teacher—A Memoir." *Pembroke Magazine* 13 (1981): 87–89.

Owen, Guy. "Postscript: American Poetry in the 60s." In *Modern American Poetry: Essays in Criticism,* ed. Guy Owen, 253–62. Deland, FL: Everett/Edwards, 1972.

———. Review of *Helmets,* by James Dickey. *Southern Poetry Review* 5, no. 1 (1964): 34.

———. "The Teacher, the Poet, and the Little Magazine." *Furman Studies* 14, no. 4 (1967): 1–13.

Owen, Guy, and Mary C. Williams. Introduction. In *Contemporary Southern Poetry: An Anthology,* ed. Guy Owen and Mary C. Williams, xvii–xxiii. Baton Rouge: Louisiana State UP, 1979.

"Poetry Review a Coup for City." Editorial. *Charlotte Observer,* 17 August 1977.

Rubin, Louis D., Jr. Introduction. In *New Southern Poets,* ed. Guy Owen and Mary C. Williams, xii–xiv. Chapel Hill: University of North Carolina Press, 1974.

Walter, Thomas N. "A Tribute to Guy Owen." *Southern Poetry Review* 21, no. 2 (1981): 8–10.

Williams, Mary C. "Guy Owen and *SPR.*" *Southern Poetry Review* 21, no. 2 (1981): 10–11.

Don't Leave Hungry

1

The Late 1950s
and the 1960s

From the late 1950s through the 1960s, Guy Owen shaped his journal's identity, and so it is fitting how often poems about identity and boundaries show up in its pages during these years (see Ammons's "Periphery" and Brosman's "A Question of Identity" in this section). The journal evolved during one of the most tumultuous eras in the modern life of America and reflected it. The country's "identity crisis" involved far too many variables to enumerate here, much less to discuss, but a quick list catches the discontent and upheaval of the time: the ongoing Cold War and accelerating arms race, the Viet Nam War, various "rights" movements, the explosion of a "counterculture" that questioned all forms of "Establishment." (Cultural anxieties show up explicitly in Sange's "Deliveries from Viet Nam" and Berry's "To My Children, Fearing for Them.") Boundaries expanded in other ways, as well. Television supplanted radio. Rock-and-roll took the throne, and the British invaded with the Beatles. IBM developed the first computer language, Xerox its first office copier. Humans walked on the moon.

American poetry tested its boundaries, too, and in doing so, affected poetry all over the world. "Free verse" was not new, of course, but it became a rocket in this era, fueled in large part by "Confessional" poetry, as well as various other "schools": Beat, New York, Deep Image, Black Mountain. Guy Owen questioned the New Critical, formalist stances, too, although he valued both, to a point. This section opens with his sonnet "Praise be to Eve," but its inclusion should not typecast him. Instead, it reminds one that, as an editor, especially during the exploratory zeal of the 1960s, Owen held no exclusive allegiances; throughout his tenure he published more "free verse" than formal. The section ends with "A Family Romance" by Howard Nemerov, another formalist by training, who chooses sometimes to mute that training for effect, as in this poem. As bookends, Owen and Nemerov represent contradictory impulses within poetry during this time, as well as within American culture, suggesting that Owen's journal took full measure of them. Of course, what these bookends hold between them in the section cannot be neatly summarized, but the surprises and pleasures there affirm Owen's vision for the journal.

GUY OWEN

Praise be to Eve

Praise be to Eve for season's gifts,
For leaves of blood and sudden drifts
Of healing snow: a fortunate fall,
Bequeathing us this miracle.

The hand that reached the tallest fruit
Gathered the winds and scattered sleet,
Unholy rime and sullen ice
To trumpet the walls of paradise.

That ragged core she nibbled on
Trembled the garden into stone,
And from that dark and fated seed
Sprang the willow, mounted the weed,

All things proud, strange, perverse—
All beauty born beneath the curse.

JAMES DICKEY

The Falls

Upon the light, bare, breathless water
To step, and thereby be given a skiff
That hangs by its nose to the bank
And trembles backward:

To stand on those boards like a prince
Whose kingdom is still as a cloud,
And through it, like a road through Heaven,
The river moves:

To sink to the floor of the boat
As into a deep, straining coffin,
And in one motion come from my mother,
Loose the long cord:

To lie here timelessly flowing
In a bed that lives like a serpent,
And thus to extend my four limbs
From the spring to the sea:

To look purely into the sky,
As the current possesses my body
Like a wind, and blows me through
Land I have walked on,

And all in a pattern laid down
By rain, and the forces of age,
Through banks of red clay, and cane-fields,
And the heart of a forest:

And at dusk to hear the far falls
Risingly roaring to meet me,
And, set in that sound, eternal
Excitement of falling:

And yet, strangely, still to be
Upheld on the road to Heaven
Through the changing, never-changed earth
Of this lived land:

And now in all ways to be drunken,
With a mind that can lift up my body
In all the grounded music of the dead
Now nearer their rising:

To do nothing but rest in my smile,
With nothing to do but go downward
Simply when water shall fall
In the mineral glimmer

Of the lightning that lies at the end
Of the wandering path of escape
Through the fields and green clouds of my birth,
And bears me on,

Ecstatic, indifferent, and
My mother's son, to where insupportable water
Shall dress me in blinding clothes
For my descent.

DALLAS WIEBE

For Jake Flickner

We go home
    to borrow money
    and bury our dead,
Counting them off
    like loose change
    into a pocket,
Jingling their names
    among our keys
    to academic offices.
Who sings of those
    named John, Jake or Pete
    after they are gone?
Their names, milled and quick,
    ring once upon a stone
    and then are spent.

X. J. KENNEDY

Edgar's Story

What we'd been missing out on, all those years
Of stoking up the coffeepot at dawn,
Those Sundays, sitting working on some beers,
Watching the sprinkler going on the lawn
Was what we wanted. Gassed the old tin can
And lit out up the turnpike, Nell and I,
Soon as I got my fourteen-karat pen
And pencil set, and wrote, and it went dry.

Woods were the good part: standing, all their limbs
Creaking with leaves. But then we'd have to go
Gawk at some china plates and hand-carved looms,
Long chains of freight cars with sad towns in tow,
And snake farms where you stood and looked at snakes.
Now, all those plastic squirrels that say, *I'm nuts
For the Dakota Bad Lands* on their butts,
That nobody laughs at, long, give me cold shakes.

Somehow, out there with not much else around,
In the motel at night, it starts to hurt,
Thinking, and your head starting to pound
In time to the drip-drying of your shirt.
You dream of redwoods melted down for pulp.
It ties a hard knot in my bowels
Every time I cost a branch to take a crap
And dry my hands off on some paper towels.

At Mount Rushmore I looked up into one
Of those faces born joined to the same neck bone.

I said, *Abe, Abe, how does it feel to be up there?*—
And that great rock he has for a pupil budged, I swear,
And he looked me right in the eye and he said, *Alone.*

Desecrations on a Theme

1.

When you are old and grey and full of sleep
And nodding by the fire, take down this book
And fling it in and let your cracked voice peep:
"So that was all he saw in me, the shnook."

2.

When forty winters have besieged thy brow
And plowed deep furrows in thy beauty's field,
Reflect: "They'd think me thirty even now
If some poetic bastard hadn't squealed."

PAUL BAKER NEWMAN

Tilghman Point

The blue-grey sound, the darker harder grey
of sea, the low faint murmur like a roll
of instants startled to quick muster by a drum
and live oaks sprung from earthworks
manned once by twenty rusty muskets and a gun.
The peaceful summers have acquired
a certain moral sanctity
through the ignorant vision of cold reeds,
conclusions or opinions reached
through rumor, nothing more,
discussions of salt wind
and sun, reports of talkative leaves
and ill-humored squabbling terns.
We climb these distances within ourselves.
The bare landscape of the marsh and tree-lined shore
creeping between the bitter alternatives of sea and land,
helps hazy predictions of the sun
fulfill their heat by noon,
the grey-green grass, the static air, the gnat-clouds
toiling like a space of time through consciousness
until the chalk-white boats command the skyline
for a moment, lost in the mesh and toiling to be still.

VASSAR MILLER

Lady of Leisure

Life never gave her any tasks
Lest labor should unnerve her.
People, she thought, were but the masks
Put on by life to serve her.

Existence was a blessed blur,
Time made a happy hum.
Waiting for life to wait on her,
She waited what might come,

And waited. Sure enough, one day,
Life, servant born and bred,
Tripped in with death upon a tray
Like John the Baptist's head.

WILLIAM MATTHEWS

The Attic, the House

People are history
but their belongings stay
around. Here Aunt Vivian

looks like a balloon.
She popped. She's dead.
The picture stays on, though,

her stretched thin smile
survived her all this while,
became her legacy.

The whole attic stinks
of permanence.
Up here my ancestry,

downstairs my tomb in preparation.
Already here some dust
has settled on me:

a baby carriage where my son
and then my cat slept
while I aged,

a baseball glove, some letters.
What's mine downstairs will soon be here,
joining the majority.

It only waits down there
in order to be me;
my favorite chair

stands stuffed, smug
as a monument, gravely
brown in its corner

about to inflate
itself
for the ascent.

The Risk

Waking up in the tawdry truth
like an old whore in her underwear:
no gaud, no carillon,
no life I'll never lead.

One foot down before the other.
Today I won't ask anyone
to love me.

JOANNE DE LONGCHAMPS

Cavafy

This I was told: a poet,
for thirty years
clerk in the Ministry of Irrigation,
an Alexandrian,
lived alone in a book-and-shadow-lined room,
telling his worry-beads,
writing by candle-light.

In the evening cafés, when he spoke
it was monologue;
gestures elaborate, open,
he scooped great ovals of air—
eyes denying what hands did;
half-shut, heavy-lidded,
they hid their suspicions,
their hungry black-blazing.

He is dead and you travel the sweep of his oars.
He gives you the beautiful voyage.
In a vineyard of dreams, you eat his words,
gorge on the Bacchic fruit.

Vistor to Cavafy, if you were young then,
a handsome young man—
do you remember the candle lit for you
in homage to luminous flesh
and recall the vivacious hand
shielding the ravaged face?

ANNIE DILLARD

Arches and Shadows

He proposed to me on the ferris wheel.
I nearly fell off! and once we dived
Off the board holding hands, I remember,
Though not very clearly. O it may not have been
Croquet on the lawn and twenty for dinner,
But we had our times, sir, and I had mine,
Awaiting election returns with the old crowd
Before I left. In Trieste I said Promise
You'll always love me. I actually said that.
And at the fair in Brussels I made
An extremely witty remark. A white puppy
Followed me all one afternoon, all
Around the racetrack. He promised,
He said we would live in a houseboat—
Raise ponies—sell apples—dry flowers—
All this in a peat-fire pub on Exmoor;
I was sunburned all over, even my hands.
Now in November when the cat wants out early,
It's your face I see in the folds of my dress on the chair.
I'll meet you in March in Alberta;
Today I sewed a pleat and cut a melon in your name,
Thinking: then I will travel the Great Northern Railways
And we can talk things over, sitting down.

CHARLES DAVID WRIGHT

Clearing Away

I had meant better with these boards than burning.
Bought for some purpose, then under sumac
and creeper, to mulch salamander dreams,
the bend of millipedes, the tunneling
and warp. They were a long time wasting.
Now with some show of husbandry in leather gloves
I've stopped stepping over them and cleared the yard.
That's over. Some won't burn, even that chance
lost in the slow motion of rotting. I
heap them anyway, and see beyond my elms
Rupkalvis also raking for his own
reasons. We nod. At our lines we join
piles to burn off together. It flames on
into dark and wants watching. He brings whiskey
and we sit smoking with it, feeling better.

JULIA RANDALL

A Night Song for Anne Jones

Anne, in the long night
under our hills, I think
of the long trail at the top
and you behind me in the dark.

It takes a long voice to travel
twenty years, shelter to shelter, campsite
to campsite.
They were digging Indian mounds
near Fincastle today. It is a kind
of smoke signal, that.

Last year, in the Saltville Flats—
I have lost the article—they found
a mammoth skull, a sort of bull, the same
one that's on a harp
somewhere, the British Museum, maybe.
I knew I had met that head,
Queen Shub-ad's lapis god.

I would like to think
the beast made music, and the music made
the Appalachian Trail, and that we make
somehow the footprints that will take
us off this planet, though
I will be sorry to see it go,
because I lived there once, and told
the difference between
Virginia Creeper and Poison
Ivy.

Now I am getting old,
these vines are dear to me
as to Shub-ad her gold. I cannot face
loving beyond a place.
I only pray,
loving this night of my life, becoming day,
that that is what we are meant to do.
I have burned no bushes behind me. But maybe you
can pick up the trail. It is never lonely. See,
green, gold, the weathers grow. They are not falling.
And listen! From every glen
the neighbor tongues with one pure voice are telling
how the heart is home, is at home in the long climbing,
how it has reached
already by every needle it has touched,
rough rock and lichen,
the simple all-tenanted kingdom
of its long peace.

A. R. AMMONS

Periphery

One day I complained about the periphery
that it was thickets hard to get around in
    or get around for
an older man: it's like keeping charts

of symptoms, every reality a symptom
where the ailment's not nailed down:
    much knowledge, precise enough,
but so multiple it says this man is alive

or isn't: it's like all of a body answering
all of pharmacopoeia, a too
    adequate relationship:
so I complained and said maybe I'd brush

deeper and see what was pushing all this
periphery, so difficult to make any sense
    out of, out:
with me, decision brings its own

hesitation: a symptom, no doubt, but open
and meaningless enough without paradigm:
    but hesitation
can be all right, too: I came on a spruce

thicket full of elk, gushy snow-weed,
nine species of lichen, four pure white
    rocks and
several swatches of verbena near bloom.

ROBERT MORGAN

High Country

Dead springs in the hills, blue flame of sky.
The horizon goes all the way round.

When it comes the darkness sprouts from rocks and fills
the valley. Splinters of ice form in the sky,
cold air stoking light.

A crystal trills at the bottom of a well,
blasting tunnels upward.
It is the blue sun rising all night under the sea.

GARY SANGE

Office Girls

Watch and you can see
them trying to get
back to sleep all day.
One cheek heavy
on an upright fist,
eyes gone under
their own stare.
With each amorous yawn,
they stretch and succumb
to their increasingly handsome,
tall, dark
boredom.

Deliveries from Viet Nam

Pentagon officials say
"from the time of the man's death,
it takes 7 to 10 days for the remains
to reach the site of the services."
And add: "we regret this delay."

The Army Escort Booklet states
"you will be meeting persons
who are emotionally upset.
Keep your face clean-shaven,
your hair well-trimmed,
your fingernails short and clean."

With his face clean-shaven,
his hair well-trimmed,
his fingernails short and clean,
he stoops to read another direction:
HEAD. KEEP THIS END HIGH.

E. G. BURROWS

King Francis and the Maid

after Stendhal

The mirror looked.
I was sweet-talked by the liking glass.
I saw through my eyes my eyes,
allies against alas.
Pools carried my face.
Rain spread its mirrors on every dry pavement.
I sat out the sun,
sang to honor myself in the windows
that praised all angles,

and was overheard.
A man older than money
begged in false rags for his bed and lustre
the beauty I could not spare.
I saw the king through his lust and tatters,
the sere crown, the mirror
of kingdom he wore,

and knew my fraud in his glass,
in his old eyes my ravage,
poured acid over my cheeks, my eyes,
to offer myself his crone,
his raddled jill. Humble,
I burn in the blind horror of the sun.
So kingdoms crumble.

WENDELL BERRY

To My Children, Fearing for Them

Terrors are to come. The earth
is poisoned with narrow lives.
I think of you. What you will

live through, or perish by, eats
at my heart. What have I done? I
need better answers than there are

to the pain of coming to see
what was done in blindness,
loving what I cannot save. Nor,

your eyes turning toward me,
can I wish your lives unmade
though the pain of them is on me.

ROBERT WATSON

Two Old People

Let the houses fall.
Let them flick down those that choose
To stand in the brash wind.
Help the wind blow the whole town down
To a rubbish heap.

Send the Mayor matches.
Let him light the pile.
Let them dance around the flames
Until the wind has twirled the town away.

Let us, backs to the light of the fire,
Read some book against wind,
Against fire,
Pranks.

Let us read a book
Old, awkward, tedious as we
To hold against the clever wind.

Let us read a story
Of a man, a woman
Who built a house
That men and wind and fire conspired against.

A story of a man, a woman
Who reading a book
Yawn
Into the straight, steady rain

Of sleep, a rain of a late autumn
Day with nothing to do
But watch the fire purring in the fireplace.

LARRY RUBIN

The Sons

There was great relief at his funeral.
We had all murdered him with promises
Of love, and no one had caught us—
The perfect crime, we thought, feeling
Our new identities like holy robes.
Mother was so radiant in black—
Reborn (we thought), an earnest of our
Immortality; she would grace us
Into heaven, pleading pardon for
Our sins. Her look of grief would pass.
                                 Too soon
The cortege fled—the bearers paid, the flowers
Shrinking into the grave. And suddenly
The magic of death was over—only the mound
Remained, like a ground swell in the earth,
A throb in nature. And as we turned to go,
Mother looked much older. Her breasts were gone,
Her face a warp behind the veil. She fell
Upon his clay, whispering (we thought)
The promises.
                  Then we heard the curse.

HEATHER ROSS MILLER

The Comet

Thrusting west,
Bright hairs combed out in a tail,
The comet appeared, just visible,
Over the beam of the barn.
It had no business
Flicking so nervously in the dark
And scattering fiery hairs all over our yard.
And neither had you any business sitting there
So primly in the black grass,
Your sharp bright face
Sighted westward,
Up skyward,
Watching that comet usurp the sky.

Strangers appear.
They get themselves born in country beds
And are christened.
Comets, without warning, seize the sky
Late a country evening,
While potatoes still bubble in the pot.
And late a country evening,
You watch the fiery sky
And read a language written
For your nebulous eye.

DABNEY STUART

The Warehouse Chute

As a boy I started at the top,
Sixth floor, as high as my father's business
Reached, a sort of skyline
In a squat and stolid city
Where men moved among goods, and knew
Themselves as the goods moved, always down.
But that was their concern
And none of my business.
Seated on cardboard or wax paper
I spiraled that metal slide
Past every merchandise
At jerkneck speed, and didn't care
If I never stopped, because
I knew I would—come to the smooth
Bright easy finish of that ride.

I never needed Vergil
Or thought of him, but now
That place seems hell enough—
A house of wares which never spoke
A word, or sang a song,
Yet held its men, my father
And his father, as a sorcerer
Enthralls a knight,
Benights an age, held them
And made them move
As it would have them move,
In darkness and in circles,
Wearing them empty as that chute—

Seems hell enough.
Now in my dreams the spiral
Spirals without end.
I see myself on every level
Smiled at by a carton,
Never Beatrice, smiled at
By this past that hands me on,
Guideless, always going down.

COLEMAN BARKS

Goat & Boy

rocking motion of remembering: red pig-iron gate latch
now my feet are on the tree roots   just inside the fence
hyaah hyaaah to scare him away   like I've seen done
this goat with eyes broken red inside   his head even
with mine   the horns glance off my shoulder into ivy
the screen door that I run to   is locked from inside
a hoof on the step behind me   then his goatface dressed
in a strand of ivy   waiting for me to take hold of
years ridged into horn   conch shell in my hands
slowly rocking side to side   neither of us with arms
deadlocked in a zodiac of child & goat   a period piece
without a sound or a cry   but moving on its own

CATHARINE SAVAGE BROSMAN

A Question of Identity

See how the shore receded in the dark
as the tide rose: tracks of crabs
which we came to read, moon-pulled, at midnight

become cuneiform on the sea floor;
waves wash the flank of the road
and patches of grass are swallowed in the sway,

sway of water, the bubbly wreaths
visited on the drowned. Boundaries seem too
uncertain: overnight the line can change

between the loose, terrible sea
which can pull my legs out in the undertow
and the sands where I have taken hold.

My dreams of drowning revive: I can already
feel the breakers beating at my bones; old
live oaks may succumb at last to liquid.

Are all our questions still to be re-asked?
perhaps the very dryness of the land,
the wetness of the wet called into doubt?

But wait: the tide turns, and the zenith sun
sheds demarcation on the shore,
and the changing wind says   that this

is the truth of the bay:
all things must have an edge, keeping
identity, however tenuous; even space

that crashes into gaseous ruffs of stars;
oceans exhausting themselves
in shallow inlets; even a storm which is turned

back, as the trees resist. And that the ends
of things, stream, continent, or a love
splintering against a sandbar

—all peripheries—are, in their dual light,
also the center of reality—since
we know the world by differences,

the sea by the way it floods a shelf of beach,
and the wind, by its dervish shape
among antennaed dunes.

PAUL RAMSEY

Yvor Winters

High and cold that air! High and cold
"From a great distance" looking forth
("From a great distance" is his phrase)
from a mountain downward, standing
stiff in that world of obscure mists,
of hard trails vanishing upwards
which he has in violence climbed
and is sick of violence, sick
of fever, of the wild caring
of plenteous youth, there he stands.
Wisdom is his name for the place,
a place of bitterness, longing,
nostalgia, perfected anger,
of cost, careful understanding,
of emotions trained like watch dogs,
still fierce in their nature, restrained,
yet fierce, strong, manful, and hostile.
And tender. Tender sometimes. Tender
towards those who face the journey
which is a hard journey upward
where old campfires darken, darken,
the flowers thin out gradually
beside the trail. In the slow mist
there are many places to fall.
Many have fallen. Reflect, then,
on the nature of falling. Reason.
Defend the high and cold summit.

JEAN FARLEY

Language of Flowers

The finest flowers of the grave
Are plastic roses so firmly red
They never curl or crave
Any commerce with the dead;

Nor privately leach their strength
To divide and glory and multiply
From the works of that swollen trench
Too easily pierced by the mourner's eye.

Steadfast and incorruptibly pure,
They advise all summer long
Of the death which living flesh obscured:
The shameful flowering now is gone.

HOWARD NEMEROV

A Family Romance

Lovers everywhere are bringing babies into the world.
Lovers with stars in their eyes are turning the stars
Into babies, lovers reading the instructions in comic books
Are turning out babies according to the instructions; this
Progression is said by demographers to be geometric and
Accelerating the rate of its acceleration. Lovers abed
Read up the demographers' reports, and accordingly produce
Babies with contact lenses and babies diapered in the flags
Of new and underdeveloped nations. Some experts contend
That bayonets are being put in the hands of babies
Not old enough to understand their use. And in the U.S.,
Treasury officials have expressed their grave concern about
The unauthorized entry of stateless babies without
Passports and knowing no English: these "wetbacks,"
As they are called from the circumstances of their swimming
Into this country, are to be reported to the proper
Authority wherever they occur and put through channels
For deportation to Abysmo the equatorial paradise
Believed to be their country of origin—"where,"
According to one of our usually unformed sorcerers,
"The bounteous foison of untilled Nature alone
Will rain upon the heads of these homeless, unhappy
And helpless beings apples, melons, honey, nuts, and gum
Sufficient to preserve them in their prelapsarian state
Under the benign stare of Our Lord Et Cetera forevermore."

Meanwhile I forgot to tell you, back at the ranch,
The lovers are growing older, becoming more responsible.
Beginning with the mortal courtship of the Emerald Goddess

By Doctor Wasp—both of them twelve feet high
And insatiable; he wins her love by scientific means
And she has him immolated in a specially designed mole—
They have now settled down in an L-shaped ranch-type home
Where they are running a baby ranch and bringing up
Powerful babies able to defend their Way of Life
To the death if necessary. Of such breeding pairs
The average he owns seven and a half pairs of pants,
While she generally has three girdles and a stove.

They keep a small pump-action repeater in the closet,
And it will not go off in the last act of this epic.

To sum up, it was for all the world as if one had said
Increase! Be fruitful! Multiply! Divide!
Be as the sands of the sea, the stars of the firmament,
The moral law within, the number of molecules
In the unabridged dictionary. BVD. Amen. Ahem
                                        AUM.
(Or, roughly, the peace that passeth understanding).

2

The 1970s

Throughout the 1960s *Southern Poetry Review* sought and fashioned its identity. In the 1970s, the journal found its confident stride. Issue after issue, one marvels over consistently strong poems. Writers who will become "big" names in the world of American poetry show up here early in their careers: Henry Taylor, Carolyn Kizer, Charles Wright, Stephen Dunn, all go on to win the Pulitzer Prize. In a significant twist, Fred Chappell's masterful *Midquest* and John Ashbery's *Self-Portrait in a Convex Mirror* share the Bollingen Prize in 1985. (Several poems from *Midquest* first appeared in *SPR* in the 1970s.) Billy Collins will become a bestseller, a "popular" poet not diminished by that term. But poems by lesser-known or "unknown" poets from this era dazzle, too, and who can say now how their futures will fare? Owen was out to print the best he could find, wherever he found it. He remained editor for most of the decade, officially turning *SPR* over to Robert Grey and a new staff in 1978.

During this period, he realized his ideal of an "eclectic" approach, selecting poetry from the South, for sure, but also from the West Coast, the Northeast, and just about everywhere in between. He pushed readers to avoid regionalism, at the same time that he championed a region, and he included work with international influence (see David Kirby's "Letter to Borges," Adrianne Marcus's "Lines After Larkin: The Pornographic Movie," Charles Wright's "6 Lines for Chi K'ang") to keep the picture even bigger. Too, although he relished Robert Morgan's poems of remote Appalachia, he did not shy from Turner Cassity's "The New Dolores Leather Bar." He sought out powerful women's voices and those of black experience (see Gerald W. Barrax's "In the Restaurant"), urban voices, voices of Jewish experience, the homespun (see Juanita Tobin's "Crazy Tuttle"), the intellectual. Owen's editorial style was exuberantly inclusive.

One notices the large scale of so much in American life in the 1970s. Disney World opens, Watergate breaks, Nixon resigns, the Viet Nam War ends, Hollywood scores with "blockbusters," disco throbs loudly, Israel and Egypt sign the Peace Treaty. The EPA forms in 1970, but the country is forced to contemplate world "ecology" because of (among other things) oil crises early and late in the decade. The economy is at its worst since the Depression: double-digit interest rates. Heiress Patricia Hearst is kidnapped, sort of. Tom Wolfe coined the phrase "the Me Decade" for the 1970s, and perhaps our current culture of public exposure began with "streaking" and Confessional poetry, but the times never overpowered Owen's journal.

Somehow, *Southern Poetry Review* kept its center. The poem that opens this section, Henry Taylor's "The Flying Change," perfectly models the willingness to experiment that Owen valued, as well as his own traditional impulses as an editor. The section ends with William Stafford's wonderfully quiet and introspective poem, "Mother Talking in the Porch Swing." An antidote to a "Me" generation, it concludes with a river "trying to give away everything, everything."

HENRY TAYLOR

The Flying Change

1.

The canter has two stride patterns, one on the right lead and
one on the left, each a mirror image of the other. The leading
foreleg is the last to touch the ground before the moment of
suspension in the air. On cantered curves, the horse tends to
lead with the inside leg. Turning at liberty, he can change leads
without effort during the moment of suspension, but a rider's
weight makes this more difficult. The aim of teaching a horse to
move beneath you is to remind him how he moved when he was
free.

2.

A single leaf turns sideways in the wind
in time to save a remnant of the day;
I am lifted like a whipcrack to the moves
I studied on that barbered stretch of ground,
before I schooled myself to drift away

from skills I still possess, but must outlive.
Sometimes when I cup water in my hands
and watch it slip away and disappear,
I see that age will make my hands a sieve;
but for a moment the shifting world suspends

its flight and leans toward the sun once more,
as if to interrupt its mindless plunge
through works and days that will not come again.

I hold myself immobile in bright air,
sustained in time astride the flying change.

The Muse Once More

> I take the air, the sun,
my ease, letting things go for a while, as the dog
> blunders from my feet to the curb and back.
> The words in the book I am holding recede,
> waver into illegibility; the air
> trembles with jet planes, birds invade;
>> it is one of those days

>> when nothing at all
can go wrong. Across the way, I see my neighbor
> lurching onto his lawn with some machine—
> a rug shampooer? No, he straps a box
> to his side, fastens earphones to his head,
> and walks his lawn, sweeping before him
>> the sensitive disc

>> of a metal detector.
What in God's name is he looking for? It is ten-thirty;
> he ought to be at work. But neither am I,
> so I do not hail him. Back and forth,
> back and forth he trudges over the spongy grass,
> swinging the handle, his head cocked for
>> a signal whose meaning

>> I cannot guess. A lost
earring, perhaps, or the tap to the water meter;
> no relics lie in this developed earth.
> The sun moves higher overhead; he sweats,
> walks on, and in my own head I begin

to carry that heavy intentness,
            waiting for the whine

            that will let me know
I have struck—what? The cars pass on their various
    errands, snapping the asphalt bubbles,
    and I doze here, dreaming that something lies
    under a suburban lawn, waiting to change
    my life, to draw me away from what
            I chose too long ago

            to forsake it now,
on some journey out of legend, to smuggle across
    the world's best-guarded borders this token,
    whatever it is, that says *I have risked*
    my life for this moment; do not forget me.
    Whatever this makes me, accept it;
            by this let me be known.

            And my neighbor walks on,
hunting the emblem that will tell him who he is now
    or might once have become. I will not wait
    to watch him find it; let it be the lost
    treasure that turns his head on the pillow
    as he drifts, as I do, toward sleep,
            out of the life he has chosen.

DENISE LEVERTOV

Heights, Depths, Silence, Unceasing Sound of the Surf

Are they birds or butterflies?
They are sailing, two, not a flock,
more silver-white than the high
clouds, blissful
solitary lovers in infinite azure.

Below them, within the reef,
green shallows, transparent.
                              Beyond,
bounded by angry lace that
flails the coral,
                  the vast,
ironic dark Pacific.

Tonga, March 17, 1979

JIM WAYNE MILLER

How America Came to the Mountains

"Brier" is the name applied, in a cycle of "ethnic" jokes, to Southern Appalachian
people who migrate to midwestern and northern industrial centers.

The way the Brier remembers it, folks weren't sure
at first what was coming. The air felt strange,
and smelled of blasting powder, carbide, diesel fumes.
A hen crowed and a witty prophesied
eight lanes of fogged-in asphalt filled with headlights.
Most people hadn't gone to bed that evening,
believing an awful storm was coming into the mountains.

And come it did. At first, the Brier remembers,
it sounded like a train whistle far off in the night.
They felt it shake the ground as it came roaring.
Then it was big trucks roaring down an interstate,
a singing like a circle saw in oak,
a roil of every kind of noise, factory
whistles, cows bellowing, a caravan
of camper trucks bearing down
blowing their horns and playing loud tapedecks.

He recollects it followed creeks and roadbeds
and when it hit, it blew the tops off houses,
shook people out of bed, exposing them
to a sudden black sky wide as eight lanes of asphalt,
and dropped a hail of beer cans, buckets
and bottles clattering on their sleepy heads.
Children were sucked up and never seen again.

The Brier remembers the sky full of trucks
and flying radios, bicycles and tv sets, whirling
log chains, red wagons, new shoes and tangerines.
Others told him they saw it coming like a wave
of tumbling dirt and rocks and car bodies
rolling before the blade of bulldozer,
saw it pass on by, leaving a wake
of singing commercials, leaving ditches
full of spray cans and junk tires, canned
biscuit containers, tinfoil pie plates.
Some told him it fell like a flooding creek
that leaves ribbons of polyethylene
hanging from willow trees along the bank
and rusty car doors half-silted over on sandbars.

It was that storm that dropped beat-up cars
all up and down the hollers, out in fields
just like a tornado that tears tin sheets
off tops of barns and drapes them like scarves
on trees in quiet fields two miles from any settlement.
And that's why now so many old barn doors
up and down the mountains hang by one hinge
and gravel in the creek is broken glass.

That's how the Brier remembers America coming
to the mountains. He was just a little feller
then but he recollects how his Mama got
all of the younguns out of bed, recalls
being scared of the dark and the coming roar
and trying to put both feet into one leg
of his overalls.
        They left the mountains fast
and lived in Is, Illinois for a while
but found it dull country and moved back.
The Brier's lived in As If, Kentucky ever since.

DAVID KIRBY

Letter to Borges

Dear Sir: you don't know me but that's not the point.
I have an idea which I think you can use.
It's not my idea anyway. Here it is:
last night my four-year-old son explained to me,
with perfect conviction, that the First Man and Woman
were actually named Wayne and Wanda
rather than Adam and Eve. Think of it, sir:
as the author of "Pierre Menard, Author of *Don Quixote*,"
in which you describe that friend of yours
who composed "not another *Don Quixote*—
which would be easy—but *the Don Quixote*,"
by which act of deliberate anachronism
and erroneous attribution he enriched
the hesitant and rudimentary art of reading,
surely you can imagine a world in which, for instance,
Napoleon might be named Waldo Davenport
and Caesar would turn out to be Bertram T. Watkins III.
And what if God himself were named Bubba or Buddy?
When people prayed, instead of saying
"Almighty God, we implore thee,"
they would say "Hey, Bubba!" And other people would say
"His name's not Bubba, stupid, it's Buddy!"
and that would be one difference right there.
Of course, you would want all the names to change
at one time, see: everyone would wake up
and all the famous people would have silly names
and vice versa. Think of the fun of it, sir! And the justice.

TURNER CASSITY

The New Dolores Leather Bar

> *I adjure thee, respond from thine altars,*
> > *Our Lady of Pain.*
> > > —A. C. Swinburne

Not quite alone from night to night you'll find them.
Who need so many shackles to remind them
Must doubt that they are prisoners of love.

The leather creaks; studs shine; the chain mail jingles.
Shoulders act as other forms of bangles
In a taste where push has come to shove.

So far from hardhats and so near to Ziegfeld,
They, their costume, fail. Trees felled, each twig felled,
One sees the forest: Redneck Riding Hood's.

Does better-dear-to-eat-you drag, with basket,
Make the question moot? Go on and ask it.
Red, do you deliver, warm, the goods?

Or is the axle-grease, so butch an aura,
Underneath your nails in fact mascara?
Caution, lest your lie, your skin unscarred,

Profane these clanking precincts of the pain queen.
Numb with youth, an amateur procaine queen,
In the rite you lose the passage. Hard,

To know the hurt the knowledge. Command is late now,
Any offer master of your fate now.
You can, though won't, escape. Tarnishing whore,

So cheap your metal and so thin your armor,
Fifteen years will have you once more farmer.
Mammon values; earth and pain ignore.
Name your price and serve him well before.

Adding Rattles

The season turns, and to its chillest blood
Bears witness that a skin must soon be shed:
The rounding self forsaken; with its scars,
Its old concealments worn to use, be lost
Also our shining tread that knows the earth.
Another year of clarities and shade
Requires its other dazzle to conceal,
And on our back the diamonds are fresh.
Old Belly, can you learn again the ways
Effaced? And you, Blood each time more enclosed,
Can you account it, in so hard rebirth,
All gain that you should see beside you, stiff
In death and in this wisest light transparent,
What you were? Who gain here otherwise
(Warm!) no envelopment not still to lose,
And one more sound to warn each touch away.

CHARLES WRIGHT

6 Lines for Chi K'ang

My thoughts, which should wander like match lights
in the Great Void,
turn back to the mountains
and lie in the shadowed snarl of the blackberry vines.
Whatever it was I wanted is still there,
                              footmarks on the wet leaves.

November

Across the river, the sun, rim-barbed,
Blood spot on the sky's bandage, burns in its ecstasy;
Corn stalks give in to the year's windfall.

Life, once coiled like a rope on the back porch,
Shakes loose, short as a shoestring,
The sound of ground leaves, Old Nothing loading his pipe.

Venetian Spring

The peach blooms,
                        words are a house of rain.

Fire dogs, ashes, the soap of another life,
Whatever is due me still
I give it back.

                        And this hive
Of emptiness, this wax in its little box.

SHARON OLDS

The Domesticators

L. O. C. (1909–1976)

This daughter, 67, who looked
so much like her mother, 93—
the same inverted rainbow smile
they paint on the sweet faces of dolls—
two years later to the day has also vanished.

She went into the closet to change,
wearing an old floral-print dress
with a diamond pin, and when he looked for her
hours later, he found nothing. Only
dark pairs of shoes like the halves of shells,
and that body on the bed.

When ladies of this sweetness go,
it almost makes it seem safe,
so decorously they dismount, leaving
the beast on the bed, quietly going
into the closet privately
to change.

FRED CHAPPELL

Dawn Wind Unlocks the River Sky

Early half-light, dawnwind driving
The trees.
              Wind ravels the scribble of vague clouds,
Fingers the Primavera glass curtain at sill-corner and bellies
It forward, here is my galleon-sail, I can voyage where I whither;
And do not. I push more deeply my face,
Love, to your breast.
Your small breathing harbors me. *Bedroom curls and uncurls*
              with breath.
Just as the curtain curling, uncurling, is free to voyage in arabesque,
Not leaving its true place. The small breathing of earth
In our window delivers me the houses and trees, souls aswoon
              in wind,
Spirits drifting on the dawnwind like sleep-smoke, bonfire
Smoke.
        First sun in the glass curtain dyes it with fire,
                 It is a fire in air,
      It is a fanfare of pure spirit, prelude, aubade.

                           Do I now
Desire you harshly?
No, it is the false desire of fresh morning, my body seeks limit
Merely, curb and margin, wind-plunged.
It is a half-bitter floating in this sea of spirit,

This sea of music,
Passacaglia to every ocean, I am swimming your skin
Of touchless fire and earth-salt. Wind drives me forward like
The spider's doily, anchored at corner and corner and corner to the

Domestic shapes: black hairbrush like a sea urchin, cologne bottle,
Hairpins and comb, deodorant can,
The mirror like a burning window.
                              (Bedroom fills now
                    With the duet—Rossini—of blue jay and stinksparrow.)

                         How the world was formed:
Wind huddled together from every quarter the dead men in it,
Wistful spirits in a gang chained lamenting to the elements,
     Elements carried from the Four Quarters by the old East Wind,
By Auster, and Zephyr,
And by rapacious snaketailed Boreas.
Suffering of spirit, suffering of elements,
In one mass.

                    My birthday, Year Thirty-Five,
May 28, 1971,
Is tumbling the dawn awkwardly as a broken boxkite, slenderest
                    of twines
Holds it to me, it is Anybody's Birthday, the whole world is
                    born again
In the morning flush of loosed wind-spirit, exhalation
Of fire-seed and gusty waters and of every dirt, Birthday sails
                    on streams
Of atoms, freshening now the breeze in the Solomons and by
                    Greenland,
Brilliantly invading the spicy Virgins.

Fire coming apart now to wind, earth
Divides to rivers, the world of waking shoves me bodyward.
How may I retrieve my spirit where it twirls
In the glasswalled caves of wind? Speech of morning,
Dawnwind driving the trees sunward, it is
Your breath, love, caught back pulsing in your throat where
                    you swim
In the spirit sea, where the inspiration of your bright hair

Flows on the pillow, your bright hair a river
Of fire in early sunlight.
                              The pillowslip blood-warm
With breath, the little flame of blood kindles the bedroom.

                              I rock now out of the air, out
Of the pure music of absence. In the companioned bed
I retake my body, May 28, 1971.
                                        Time   time   time

To rise.
Put your pants on, Birthday Boy, the trees are
Wide awake. The shining net of dream plunges to earth,

Earth rises out of air to greet my flesh.

SUSAN LUDVIGSON

Trainer's Temper Bars Him from His Beloved Elephants

Headline, *The Charlotte Observer*

All day when one is giving birth
you sweat, roll on the ground,
clenching your knees to your belly.
At night you lie beside her
groaning, as she bellows pain,
humiliation, to the stars.
You understand the language.
When you sleep on the ground
you feel it shudder
with the memory of a herd
turning the grassy plain
to dust. When you bring straw
you want to spin it gold,
to make vast brocade blankets
and a shimmering jacket for yourself.

But when the youngest refuses
to eat, you smash the bottle
on his soft head, claiming
an accident. Sometimes
when they cry all night
for nothing, you take a fat stick
and let them know whose word
is law. They never blame you,
but tremble in the corners
while you croon.

Your father wept
each time he bruised you.
Once you went to school
with a broken arm
and when you got home
he twisted it, so you'd
remember. When he died
you stayed at the grave
five days in the rain,
still hearing his words:
We're all beasts, son.
Trust no one.
Do not marry.
Do not have children.
Nobody understands
the nature of love.

W. S. DOXEY

My Father's Friends

In those houses of glass
My father walked up and down
Speaking to them of rain,
Of sun, of the distant lands
From which he brought them home.
In the moisture pools underneath
The benches fish made lazy circles.
And my father crunched up and down
On the damp gravel pathway
Sweating through his khakis
Speaking in the same patient tone.
The orchids never spoke back;
But at certain moonstruck intervals
They opened up and bloomed.

LINDA PASTAN

Drift

Lying in bed this morning
you read to me of continental drift,
how Africa and South America
sleeping once side by side
slowly slid apart;
how California even now
pushes off like a swimmer
from the country's edge, along
the San Andreas Fault.
And I thought about you and me
who move in sleep each night
to the far reaches of the bed,
ranges of blanket between us.
It is natural law this drift
and though we break it
as we break bread
over and over again, you remain
Africa with your deep shade,
your heat. And I, like California,
push off from your side
my two feet cold
against your back, dreaming
of Asia Minor.

JULIE SUK

Seeds

I halve an apple on the radius
and discover a star-shaped center.
At the flowering end of the apple
you see the same star
only pulled in
the way a turtle snaps back
frightened
into puckered skin

the way we clutch what we own
don't touch! don't touch!
as if this was likely
preserved as we are
and swathed to death.

But this inner star is open
full of seeds
jumbled like miniature boats
robbed and left in an ancient tomb
long since forgotten.

Everywhere hunger.

Ferryboat seeds going out
coming back
oarless

the life inside
waiting to be rescued.

WILL WELLS

Vertigo

Like a shadow, overshadowed,
I give myself to the greater dark:
the swish of cars on wet streets, the long train

passing, the voices through the wall.
As a boy I spun in a tractor tire
hung deep in the woods, and reeled home drunk

on gravity. Drawn out, drawn down,
I knew at last what drove my mother
outdoors on blizzard nights to sing

to any friend or stranger on the road.
That's how she traveled, closing her eyes,
as I do mine, turning in all directions.

DAVE SMITH

Out of the Sea, at Hatteras

For days, nothing. For days, sea-brine.

Watching waves, waiting for the graveyard
to rise, eye-sailing where the wrecks
wade through the centuries. The salty bones

in little boxes drift. They can't get away.

Spars and masts and lean ribs in blue moss,
the spines of salesmen bloodied on freeways,
stars fallen in their daughters' eyes.

Bones crossed on a median, tufts, curls flow
in sudden breeze of trucks: once a ducktail
humming Be-Bop-A-Lula.

Lulu. La la, sand sizzles, and squint
for the negative, mercury, mercurial, winged

heel: a woman's. The eternal who

hello, there. Comes, goes.
For days. You could set your clock.
Ribs well-rigged. What a pair of chines all

the way down to slop and giggle of surf. But why

this dark push of water? Forever vengeance
surely, surely, this graveyard where

just out of surf she must have come, loves
water, loves love, you can tell, always
could, way they walk. Be-Bop-A

sneer at death. Lady of the sea
if you own everything from here to Nag's Head
won't you give us a little

life: slosh in the bones, moss-moves all night
like a dancer's hair, you don't see it.

It's there. What does she care?

Oh lady won't you tell me why
your feet are green and sea-chummy?

Or if not, tell what a simple shell says.
This day is pinched, tight as a safety pin
but you know it ends and so do I.

Well, what's enough? Tell us how to be.
All we want, mother, burial and a small riff
of rain's honors.

T. R. HUMMER

Without Guilt, the Rural Carrier Reads a Postcard

They're fair game. Anyone who would write
Anything important on the back of one is a fool.
I saw one once that said, *Dear Mama: Hope you are physical.*
Also mental. Saw the reply: *I'm all right,*
Son, just the same. I lost some sleep that night
Thinking. That was years ago. Now all
I do is nod when I read them. But I read them all.
You can't make a secret of what's in plain sight.

I had an old woman on the route once who could get
Whole letters on them. Long ones. Wrote so small
I had to squint in strong sunlight to read it.
Wrote everywhere, sideways, upside-down, diagonal.
Never had much to say. But what she said
I turned sideways, upside-down, and by God read.

HEATHER McHUGH

Understanding

Bugging the upstairs parlor
where they gather I can hear
teeth rattle in glass,
the waver of voices
under water, no
olives. I can hear oranges
hiss on the women's lips,
and the quick drawn
little blues, the breath
of lighters. Smoke
makes a soft white sound.
The wall trembles like a tympanum.
All at once, too near
in the dark beneath the floor
some cellar presence—root,
foot—makes it move.
My bones crawl together from corners.
My ears curl back to my skull.
I am in time, almost: a hand's
upon a wrist. It's mine.

Cool

The air no longer glues
to my skin. Commotion,
that slow burn, is far gone.

It is late summer, late
afternoon; between this day-
room and the passion of dogs
and horns a hundred
years have intervened, a single shade
of stripe and sun, of swell
and sink. In the garden
are no small shaking
bells, no verdure, syrups, purple
vibes, no humming promises, no rings.
The empty garden is an attitude
of rocks, and I have made
my peace with the planted
stone. Already I lie in the box

of my house and love
you for leaving
me free
of all sweetness and sting.

JOHN STONE

He Makes a House Call

Six, seven years ago
when you began to begin to faint
I painted your leg with iodine

threaded the artery
with the needle and then the tube
pumped your heart with dye enough

to see the valve
almost closed with stone.
We were both under pressure.

Today, in your garden,
kneeling under the sticky fig tree
for tomatoes

I keep remembering your blood.
Seven, it was. I was just
beginning to learn the heart

inside out.
Afterward, your surgery
and the precise valve of steel

and plastic that still pops and clicks
inside like a ping-pong ball.
I should try

chewing tobacco sometime
if only to see how it tastes.
There is a trace of it at the corner

of your leathery smile
which insists that I see inside
the house: someone named Bill I'm supposed

to know; the royal plastic soldier
whose body fills with whiskey
and marches on a music box

How Dry I Am;
the illuminated 3-D Christ who turns
into Mary from different angles;

the watery basement,
the pills you take, the ivy
that may grow around the ceiling

if it must. Here, you
are in charge—of figs, beans,
tomatoes, life.

At the hospital, a thousand times
I have heard your heart valve open, close.
I know how clumsy it is.

But health is whatever works
and for as long. I keep thinking
of seven years without a faint

on my way to the car
loaded, loaded with vegetables,
I keep thinking of seven years ago

when you bled in my hands like a saint.

CAROLYN KIZER

How It Passes

for Romulus

Tomorrow I'll begin to cook like mother:
All the dishes I love, which take her
Such hours to prepare:
The easy dishes that are so difficult
Like finnan haddie and beef stew
"That I wouldn't be ashamed to serve a king";
Her applesauce, bread pudding, lemon sponge,
All the sweet nursery foods
That prove I had a happy childhood.

Starting tomorrow, I'll be brave like father,
Now that I don't have those recurring nightmares
Of jackboots on the stairs, the splintered door
                              just before dawn,
And the fascists dragging daddy out of bed,
Dragging him down the steps by his wonderful hair;
The screams as his spine cracks when he hits cement.
Then they make him brush his teeth with his own shit.
Though I know this is the price of bravery,
Of believing in justice and never telling lies,
And of being Benjamin, the best beloved.

I'll begin tomorrow. I'll learn how to work
Like my brilliant friends who speak in tongues,
Who drink and crack up, but keep on working,
While I waste my time in reading, reading, reading
The words of my brilliant and not-so-brilliant friends.

I promise to increase production, gather up
                               all those beginnings
Of abandoned novels, whose insights astound me
As I contemplate their fading paragraphs.
I'll reveal how ambitious I have been in secret!

There is plenty of time.
I'll find the starter-button soon.
After all, young women are meant to meander,
Bemused with fantasies of future loves.
It's just that I'm so sleepy tonight, so tired . . .
And when I wake up tomorrow, I'll be old.
And when night comes tomorrow
It won't go away.

SAM RAGAN

That Summer

That summer when the creeks all dried up
Except for a few deep holes
Under the caved-out roots of oaks
Now leaning toward the water's edge.
The catfish clung to the mud
But now and then a perch was caught
In the oatsack seine.
Even the Tar was a trickle
And I could walk all the way across
On the rocks, and the place
Where we had swung from limb to water,
Splashing below surface and rising sputtering,
Was now no more than moist mud
From which a turtle crawled.
        They sat on the porches
        And talked of the weather,
        And Herbert Hoover,
        Cursing both, and every son of a bitch
        Who had voted for him.
        Even if the Baptists saved any souls
        Worth the saving
        Where in the hell would they find the water
        To baptize them.
A wild turkey flew out of the woods
And even if it was out of season
He fed a family for two days.
And it was better than a mud turtle
That looked like mud and tasted like mud . . .
    that summer when it didn't rain.

GEORGE GARRETT

York Harbor Morning

Where clear air blew off the land
wind turns around and the sky changes.
Where there was burning blue is pale gray now
heavy with the salt and scent of open sea
and the lazy groaning of the foghorn
saying change   change   change
like a sleeper dreaming and breathing.

Tide turning, too, with the weather,
and the lobsterboats swing around to pull
against moorings like large dogs on chains.
Gulls cry like hurt children and vanish,
and I begin to think it was a magician,
bitter and clever, who played this trick.

That old magician is laughing in the fog.
The cries of wounded children fade away
while the bellbuoy rings farewell   farewell
daring the dead to rise from their dreaming
and hold their lives like water in their hands.

STEPHEN DUNN

The Rider

It is with me now, that falling star
that fell half way down
to Echo, Minnesota. I saw it

last night from the highway,
from a bucket seat,
a familiar wheel of comfort.

It fell fast and then stopped
the way a man falls in his dreams;
a spectacular hint of destruction

opening his eyes.

Who will believe me
if I insist
that a large man was riding it,

and the shell of a body
drove my car home into the vacancies
of garage and self,

without mishap, or a single regret?

WENDELL BERRY

Creation Myth

This is a story handed down.
It is about the old days when Bill
and Florence and a lot of their kin
lived in the little tin-roofed house
beside the woods, below the hill.
Mornings, they went up the hill
to work, Florence to the house,
the men and boys to the field.
Evenings, they all came home again.
There would be talk then and laughter
and taking of ease around the porch
while the summer night closed.
But one night, McKinley, Bill's young brother,
stayed away late, and it was dark
when he started down the hill.
Not a star shone, not a window.
What he was going down into was
the dark, only his footsteps sounding
to prove he trod the ground. And Bill
who had got up to cool himself,
thinking and smoking, leaning on
the jamb of the open front door,
heard McKinley coming down,
and heard his steps beat harder and faster
as he came, for McKinley felt the pasture's
darkness joined to all the rest
of darkness everywhere. It touched
the depths of woods and sky and grave.
In that huge dark, things that usually

stayed put might get around, as fish
in pond or slue get loose in flood.
Things could be coming close
that never had come close before.
He missed the house and went on down
and crossed the draw and pounded on
where the pasture widened on the other side,
lost then for sure. Propped in the door,
Bill heard him circling, a dark star
in the dark, breathing hard, his feet
blind on the little reality
that was left. Amused, Bill smoked
his smoke, and listened. He knew where
McKinley was, though McKinley didn't.
Bill smiled in the darkness to himself,
and let him run until his fearful steps
approached something really to fear:
the quarry pool. Bill quit his pipe
then, opened the screen, and stepped out,
barefoot, on the warm boards. "McKinley!"
he said, and laid the field out clear
under McKinley's feet, and placed
the map of it in his head.

DAVID IGNATOW

Two Untitled Poems

I.

The book flies open.
Who touched it?

The pages are flapping in the air.
Is there a wind?

The book is rising from the table.
Is it my hand?

The book is returning and has landed on my head.
The words are digging their letters into my scalp.

The book is printing itself upon my brain.
I am about to talk like a book.

I am talking like a book.
I am a book, I am a book,
and I am approaching the end.

II.

My poetry is for the night
of empty buses. I write,
depleted and hug my death.
Live for others, I hear whispered,

for the child growing,
face of a rushing stream.

I fall asleep
as if it were a poem
being written
to resolve my cares
into a final solution
and as my eyes close
and silence spreads itself
inside me like a wave
I know I am succeeding,
and in sleep rejoice.

ROBERT MORGAN

Hogpen

In the pine woods, at the log
enclosure with a roof
over one corner,
you can get up close
to the grunting breather.
And he knows you're there, always
watching through a chink.
Suddenly whirls
his great weight
squealing to the other
side, for all the size quick
as a cat, standing
in mud plush.
Living out
our exile we come as
to the oracle with offerings of
scraps, bran.
Slopped over and gomming
his snout he's after
it so fast, snorkeling
under, coughing.
Licks the trough bare to
meal stuck in the cracks,
clabber whitening
hoofpools.
Sun brews the
tincture, flies steaming.
A scree of cobs bleaches downhill
where cans of worms can

be dug every foot.
It's a good place to play on
a hot day, in the pines,
spice of hot needles,
resin swelling.
Play close to the slow
talking
panter behind the logs.
He listens, taking
an interest.
Stirs in the inner
chambers, blessing the hours.

Plankroad

Besides the Indian trails and a crude wagon trace
the first way into the mountains from the south
was a narrow gauge set of timbers on the ground
with rough boards nailed across. The clatter
of that lumber echoed off the mountains' wall
as teams and carriages from Charleston
labored up along the Saluda and into the dark
hollows, ascending out of heat. Those sleepers
rumbled like trolls under their load and
wallowed in the spring mud, drumming to the
jumpoffs and high ledges a warning: see

maples unfurl and sail on light into spring,
see higher up the oaks like ragged beggars carrying
diamonds of sap to translate into green.
The fullness has come to the cucumber trees
along the upcountry creek where floods scoured
the underbrush a few weeks ago. The new growth
tinctures light where sun has made the soil

ethereal in leaves. And solar wind takes flesh
in kalmia and chinquapin.

The millionaires from Charleston and
Atlanta built their mansions in the pines
at Flat Rock, and returned each year along
the wooden bridge to cool among the columns
and hemlocks, and worship in their private chapel.
They bought poultry and time from my forebears.
Observe the proficiency of sprouts
trading in the commissary of mud, now as
back when they grumbled from the tollhouse near
Traveler's Rest up to the Gap. Natives
walked their planks into the outlands.
The wood quickly weathered and warped where
it stilted across hungry water
and parted thickets.
The platforms snapped in cloudburst
and fungus in the lowspots ate
the flooring like venison. Then
they had their Negroes and Irishmen
dig and drag a locomotive into the mountains.

RONALD WALLACE

St. Louis Pencil Salesman Blues

Invisible until
his coughs uncover him,
he huddles in
a crevice of the city.

He keeps an office in his socks
and talks to bottles.
Time dogs him
with hungry eyes.

Children's cries
bite like fleas.
The sun
wears a blue uniform.

Clutching his bones to his neck
like a coat
he hides behind
a disguise of skin.

The nightstick wind
torments him.

ADRIANNE MARCUS

Lines After Larkin: The Pornographic Movie

Love saves us from nothing.
The tumult, impossibility
of adolescence becomes a fanciful
marriage, and in time, civility.

Passion's embarrassing as we grow
beyond it. There, on the giant screen,
a young man and woman, naked, coupling.
We sit down, amused at their fury; mean

tangle of legs, parts, nothing hidden.
Only their fixed smiles, their fused faces
tell us it's not real. Then, a stray
shadow of a cameraman places

it all in perspective. The light's
rigged. And we sigh, thankful, out
of relief and all that. Appearances
matter; we feel the years close about

us, more flesh than we wish, and settle
for subtlety, lights dimmed, the chance
we won't be condemned to replay endless
passion, failing by circumstance

of which we're the smallest part.
Like those inarticulate actors up there:
pumping and pawing reel after reel
as the audience tries not to stare.

KATHRYN STRIPLING BYER

Drought

The smell of dirt, always
the smell of dry dirt down in Georgia
where I sweated through summer,
my father complaining about the blue sky
stretching all the way west into Arkansas.
Dry ice they'd tumble
from planes sometimes. Thunder
and strong wind might come

but no rain. The pigs grumbled
from sunup to sundown. The cows stood
immobilized under the oak trees,
their turds turning black as the biscuits I burned
while I daydreamed. Where I played I saw corn dying
year after year, teased by dust devils
leaving their dust in between my toes
and in ring after ring round my neck. I scrubbed
ring after ring of black dirt from the bathtub
at night. I got used to my own sweat

and so much hot weather
the silly petunias collapsed
by mid-afternoon. Without looking I knew what
I'd find, the whole flowerbed lazy

as I was. You hold up
your shoulders straight, I heard a thousand times.
Books on my head, I'd be sent out
to water the flowers as if that would help salvage
anything but my good humor, the smell of wet dirt

my reward, for which I knew I ought
to be grateful. I am
grateful, now that I'm thirsty as dry land

I stand upon, stoop-shouldered,
wanting a flash flood to wash away Georgia
while I aim the water hose into a sad patch of pansies
as if nothing's changed. I can still hear my father complain
while my mother cooks supper and I swear to leave
home tomorrow. In Oregon dams burst
but I don't believe it. Here water is
only illusion, an old trick
light plays on the highway that runs north
through field after field after field.

MILLER WILLIAMS

Getting Experience

The first real job I got was delivering drugs
for Jarman's Pharmacy in Bascum, Arkansas.

If everyone was busy or in the back I sold things.
A cloudy woman with pentecostal hair

Softly asked for sanitary napkins.
She brought the Kleenex back unwrapped in twenty minutes.

Shame said Mr. Jarman. We shouldn't make a joke
of that and made me say I'm sorry and fired me.

When I found out what it was the woman wanted
I had to say I did what they said I did.

That or let them know I hadn't heard of Kotex.
Better be thought bad than known for stupid.

The first hard fight I had was after school
with Taylor Wardlow West in Bascum, Arkansas.

Ward West chased me home from school when I was lucky.
My father said Ward West was insecure.

Go smile at him He said and let him know
you mean to be his friend. My father believed in love.

All day I smiled and twisted in my seat to see him
all hate and slump by himself in the back of the room.

After school he sat on my chest and hit me
and then his little brother sat on my chest and hit me

and then his little sister sat on my chest and hit me.
She made me so ashamed I tried to kick her

and kicked Ward West in the face. When he could see
I was halfway home. Jesus. Jesus.

Next day everybody told me over and over
how I had balls to make those stupid faces,

him the son of a bitch of the whole school
and how I surely kicked the piss out of him.

Ward had to go to the dentist. Also his father beat him.
He didn't come to school for two days.

Then he left me alone. He said I was crazy.
Everybody thought I was a little crazy

Although with balls. I just let them say I was.
Better be thought mad than known for stupid.

Sneeze, belch or fart. Choose if you have a choice.
Nobody's going to think you're good and sane and smart.

How, Having Given Up the Classical Temper for the Romantic, We Try to Find Meaning in Death

It's hard to think the brain
a ball of ropey dough
should have posited pain
or come to know

how to distinguish legend
from life and let it go
and think we live, and imagine
that makes it so.

If these are things we lend
a fragile credence to
we come to comprehend
or think we do

how something which has the skill
to think of the mouth kissed
should lose the words and will
and not exist

or look at itself astonished
as it does now, and know
all things are good and honest
as this is so.

CHANA BLOCH

Yom Kippur

Our new clothes fool no one.
A year of days.
The fingernails keep growing,
even in life.

We are tight for the winter, brooding
in this vat of used air.
As if we could hatch
some glory out of our sitting still.

What shrinks inside us, these stones
that rattle in our throats
tell us only
to go on getting older.

But the eyes want, the fingers, the emptiness
of the mouth
wants something to speak to, some lost
horn of a mouth with its unpredictable answers.

On the eastern wall, the lions
stand on end,
raising their braided heads,
their gold tongues whetted.

A. R. AMMONS

Snow Log

Especially the fallen tree
the snow picks
out in the woods to show:

the snow means nothing by that
no special emphasis: actually
snow picks nothing out:

but was it a failure, is it,
snow's responsible for
that the brittle upright black

shrubs and small trees
set off what caught the snow
in special light:

or there's some intention
behind the snow snow's too shallow
to reckon with: I take in on myself:

especially the fallen tree
the snow picks
out in the woods to show.

JAMES SEAY

Another Sentimental Journey

Time is a tease. Time is a tease—because everything
has to happen in its own time.
                    —Nadja

Here is something from the past this morning,
outside the raised shade,
something you suppose the wind has blown
up to the French doors of the bedroom.

It is a Time-Life disc
from an ad that came in the mail,
Sentimental Journey on one side,
blank on the other,
part of an offer that there is more,
there is much much more.

If you could mend
where the dog's teeth broke through
before he dropped it at your door
(not the wind after all),
smooth the wrinkles,
and get just a snatch of what the past danced to,
wouldn't you order the whole package?

Isn't that enough—
a little teasing from Time?
You don't really want to reach out
in a past time, do you,
and find again that something

has come between your hand
and the flimsy curtain
you want to pull away?

GERALD W. BARRAX

There Was a Song

There was a song
she pulled out of the trees
as she walked her way
toes pointed slightly inward
whistling like a young boy.

There was that song
she held in her hands
that might have been the sea.
She was afraid of that,
but in her hands
it became a song, simply,
or the sound of something
without leaves or feathers.

There was she
with something of the trees
and the sea in her hands after all
and that walk that took her about the island.
    And although nobody called
    I heard her;
    although nobody called,
    I followed.

In the Restaurant

I understand
Watching this public exposure
Of mere flesh that must be fed

Why I must keep away
From the tables of my enemies
Or lose them.

Poor creatures
Betrayed by this ritual
They don't know how vulnerable we are

When their heads go down
To meet their forks
It's a gesture too much like prayer

A cry for help, a plea for kinship.
Whether something else's predator or my own enemy
Dripping the blood of a warm kill

Between the jaws of either
Death holds us closer than hate
Feeding us mortality in such small portions.

TIMOTHY STEELE

A Couple, A Domestic Interior

(on a photograph with the inscription: Vermont, 1903)

It's all in focus. The globe lamps declare
a rolltop desk and bookcase; the grained air
is still. She is sewing; he looks on,
mustached and casual—though he clearly knows
that at any moment the shutter will close.

She appears somewhat cautious, too, but why?
Nothing's out of place. Curled on the floor,
their setter; and on the far wall, his portrait
and two oval mirrors that amplify
the harmony and light. Or is there more?

A mistress in Sherbrooke? Some land deal he
pulled off to pay a gambling debt?
And on her side—a son who hates her? the
persistent fear of growing old alone?
a lover from her youth she can't forget?

Or is it merely that there's something tense
and forced about their innocence,
a willed denial of living? Still,
they look so solid, as if they knew
they'd only have to hold their pose until

the camera flashed once—and then they'd be
not simply granted security,
but fixed forever in the quiet here:
a man, a woman, a long afternoon,
calm, domestic, perfectly clear.

PHILIP APPLEMAN

Murder

Who was it standing there
while you slept? There's
a taste on the tip of the tongue
like bitter almonds, and off
in the corner of the eye
someone is slipping into dusk
at the edge of the room, and something
without a face
is chasing you through the woods, your legs
rooted like stumps,
your screaming strangled to whimpers, and
you know in the lump of your heart
that the faceless thing
is yourself, it is
man and wife slamming doors,
in the dregs of every cup
a trace of arsenic—it is rage
at the Boss, feeling
in the palm of the hand
the thump of lead pipe—it is
the fury of neighbors, the tang
of gunpowder, smell
of quicklime eating flesh: you
breathe it in with the morning
coffee, the pleasant drone
of mowing lawns,
in every blade of grass
the open razor . . .

You wrench yourself out of nightmare
and open your eyes
in time to see the bludgeon crashing down
and the face above it, roaring
with your laughter.

JUANITA TOBIN

Crazy Tuttle

Today Aunt Eunice is the only person
Living on the other side of Buckle
Except for Crazy Tuttle.
If he had a brain in his head,
It would be lonesome.
He ain't got sense enough
To pour piss out of a boot
With the directions written on the heel
Even if he did have a twenty-five year
Safety record with the bus company.
After he retired he had a vision
And saw the letters: G P C
He interpreted to mean
Go Preach Christ.
Aunt Eunice said, "Land of Goshen,
It could have meant
Go Plow Corn."

BILLY COLLINS

L'Histoire

Tiny hairs on the neck
of the French Revolution
stick up and bristle

feeling the thrill of air
before beheading.

A perfect guillotine shot
pleases the citizens
eating cheeses on the lawns.

There is nothing they enjoy more
than the swish of a falling blade
and a blue-veined sky overhead.

And now a great cheer mushrooms up
from the spectators,
those thousands of Pierres and Lucilles,

when the body lifts its head
out of the wicker basket,

dropkicks it over some hedges
and stomps off into
High Romanticism.

PHILIP DACEY

The Birthday

Thirty candles and one
to grow on. My husband
and son watch me
think of wishes.

I wish I found it
easier to make wishes
than I do. Wasn't it,
years ago, easy to make wishes?

My husband and son are wishes.
It is as if
every day I wait for them
to happen again,

and they do.
But surely there is much
I am without, yet
I stand here, wishless.

Perhaps I want
what I needn't wish for,
my life: it is
coming, everything will happen.

Or perhaps I want
precisely what I don't know,
all that darkness
so tall and handsome before me.

I have seen women age
beautifully, with a
growing, luminous
sexuality:

now I know, each year
they've been slowly
stepping out of their wishes
like their clothes.

I stand here amazed
at what is happening to me,
how I've begun to lighten
of desires, getting down

to my secret skin,
the impossibly thin
membrane this side
of nothing. Husband,

I wish I could tell you.

ELEANOR ROSS TAYLOR

Don't Leave Hungry

Don't leave hungry.
Take this bird—eat song.
This wave—drink.

Throw work out the back door
To bleach his bones.
Don't *you* do it. Play.

　　Enter night
　　Unpractised on vast scales,
　　On idle rests?

No. Lap-up the master's saucer,
Eat of this bright flesh,
Drink of this momentary blood.
All thy sins are teggen away, teggen away.

WILLIAM STAFFORD

Mother Talking in the Porch Swing

Inside the river is there a river?—
it could follow slow water the way
the real current follows a stiller
shore. And in your life the life that
hurries could pass, and pass its
open neighbor the earth, and its shore
the sky. To be here, and always to find
places in the current, the dreams
the river has—surely we bubbles
ought to tell about it?

Listen: One of the rooms the river has
after its bridge and its bend in the mountains
is a place waiting for the sun every
afternoon, when the sun dwells
at a slant under a log and finds
that little yellow room and a waterbug
trying to learn circles but never making
one its shadow approves. Miles later
the river tries to recall that dream,
turning with all of its twisting self
that found gravel and found it good.

Just before the ocean that river
turns on its back and side and slowly
invites the world and the air and the sky,
trying to give away everything, everything.

3

The 1980s

Robert Grey edited *Southern Poetry Review* from the Fall issue of 1978 until the Fall issue of 1990. Although Owen had maintained a core of staff members over the years, many people served shorter stints along the way. With fewer comings and goings, Grey's smaller main staff held in place for twelve years. Something of a North Carolina institution by 1978, the journal received support from UNC-Charlotte, where Grey taught, as well as state and NEA grants during the early and late 1980s. Grey replaced the geometric design of the retro-1960s covers with single-color card stock, alternating blue and umber for Fall and Spring issues, and he added a distinctive logo that resembled a design from the *Book of Kells*. This intricate and cryptic image promised complexity. (Owen's managing editor Mary Williams wrote that Owen never cared about covers in the least.) Grey carried his predecessor's eclectic approach into the 1980s, but he went further in making *SPR* reverberate with material from beyond the region and, most notably, beyond the country. This heightened awareness brought with it a more trenchant tone of appraisal and critique, one that holds this decade of *SPR* together.

The "Me Decade" of the 1970s spiraled into the "Greed Decade" of the 1980s. Notable figures from the era include Donald Trump and Leona Helmsley ("the Queen of Mean"). The "Greed is good" monologue in the 1987 film *Wall Street* was inspired by a real-life corporate raider. "Reaganomics" made some people rich and corporations richer. Exxon spilled a lot of oil in Alaska and groused about paying for it. Ecology? It's expensive. Singer Madonna preened as the "Material Girl." "Shop till you drop" became a 1980s mantra. Designer labels mattered, a lot. "Yuppie" entered our vocabulary.

As one might expect, poets of the era cast a cold eye on its materialism. In "Bonsai" by Jody Bolz, the speaker asks, "Why not master me, keep me / from jungling up the world, beguile / me, hold my heart still / in one small garden?" The question is clearly rhetorical. In Michael McFee's "A Tumbleweed from Texas," "relief is the sight / of someone else's / accidental fortune," an oil well's sudden geyser. But Nance Van Winckel's "Somewhere: How Can We Leave It Now?" appraises a more middle-class scenario: "To keep ourselves from going anywhere / else, we tie ourselves / to something—and look out / across our landscape of beautiful debts. . . " The oxymoron "beautiful debts" could be a logo of the era. While Bolz's poem poses a different cultural response to the material world, Edward Wilson's speaker in "For the Woman in Her Station Wagon Weeping at a Red Light" concludes, "You live in a rich country. / You have tears to spend." A startling contrast, Ed Ochester's "Mary Mihalik" commits suicide by driving her car under a moving coal truck. "People said all she needed / was a job," the speaker reports, "and I guess they're right." His "guess" suggests the answer is far more complex than that. Valuing complexity, *Southern Poetry Review* consistently published work that called the era's guiding principles into question.

Ronald Reagan served two terms as president. The Iran Hostage Crisis ended after 444 grueling days, just after Reagan took office in 1981, but the Middle East remained volatile throughout his presidency, and beyond it. Religious fundamentalism carried clout in American politics, but the Ayatollah Khomeini put a bounty on Salman Rushdie's head for writing a novel. Students protested Chinese communism in Tiananmen Square. Germans dismantled the Berlin Wall, rapturously, signaling the end of communism in Eastern Europe. "Perestroika" in Russia. The Cold War, almost over.

However, AIDS had loomed up, a pandemic by mid-decade, no end in sight. Americans were "depressed." The "Harmonic Convergence" in 1987 heralded "New Age" spiritual practices, and Prozac came on the market the same year.

A lot happened for a small poetry journal in the South to take on, or to ignore: *Southern Poetry Review* did not ignore the larger world during the 1980s, but it avoided shrill "political" poetry. Maxine Kumin's "The Poet Visits Egypt and Israel" opens this section and indicates the sort of sharp notice and diligent watchfulness of the journal during these years. As for the materialism and excess of the times, B. D. Love's "Carp," which concludes the section, assesses this age with a stoical asperity that culminates in a speech both imperious and despairing. It is not a poem of consolation, but neither is it one of surrender. The journal strove for this kind of complexity under Grey. As an editor, he appeared more of a cynic than Owen—not that every issue was morose, but he maintained this critical stance throughout his tenure. *Southern Poetry Review* in the 1980s stayed wary, in an effort to be wise.

MAXINE KUMIN

The Poet Visits Egypt and Israel

Sand, sand. In the university the halls,
seats, table tops, sills, are gritty with it.
Birds fly in and out at the open windows.
During the lecture an elderly porter
splendid in turban and djebbeleah,
shuffles in, opens a cabinet on the apron,
plugs in a microphone, spits into it twice,
and plumps it down on the lectern.
She continues to speak, amplified,

on American women poets since World War One
to an audience familiar with Dickinson,
Poe, and at a safe remove, Walt Whitman.
Afterward, thick coffee in thimbles. Sticky cakes
with the faculty. In this polite fortress
a floating unease causes her hands to shake
although nothing is said that could trespass
on her status as guest from another, unveiled, life.
She is a goddess, rich, white, American,

and a Jew. It says so in some of her poems.
There are no visible Jews in the American
Embassy, nor at the Cultural Center, and none
turns up in Cairo or Alexandria
although an itinerant rabbi is rumored
to cross from the other side once a fortnight
and serve the remaining congregants. The one
synagogue, a beige stucco Parthenon,

sleeps in the Sabbath sun, shuttered tight
and guarded by languid soldiers with bayonets.

All that she cannot say aloud she holds
hostage in her head: the congruities
of bayonets and whips; starved donkeys
and skeletal horses pulling impossible loads;
the small, indomitable Egyptian flies
that perch on lips, settle around the eyes
and will not be waved away. Like traffic
in Cairo, they persist, closing the margin
between life and death to a line so thin

as to become imperceptible.
Transported between lectures, she is tuned
to the rich variety of auto horns, each one
shriller, more cacophonous, peremptory
than its abutter. The decibel level
means everyone drives with windows closed,
tapedeck on full, airconditioning at maximum.
Thus conveyed, fender nudging fender,
she comes to ancient Heliopolis

where the Sheraton sits apart in an oasis.
Gaudier than Las Vegas, she thinks, checking in.
Behind her in the lobby, two BMWs,
several sheiks, exotic birds in cages,
and plumbing fixtures of alabaster
ornament this *nouveau riche* heaven.
Backlighted to enhance their translucency,
the toilet tank and bidet bowl are radiant,
the kind of kitsch she wishes she didn't notice.

Outdoors in the sports enclave, pool attendants
in monogrammed turtlenecks, like prep-school athletes,
carry iced salvers from bar to umbrellaed table,

proffer thick towels, reposition chaises longues
for the oiled, bikinied, all-but-naked bodies
of salesmen's wives and hostesses on holdover.
What do they think about, the poet wonders,
as they glide among the infidels, these men
whose own wives wrap up head to toe in public,

whose cousins creep from day to day
in a state of chronic lowgrade emergency.
Anonymous again in transit,
the poet leaves for Tel Aviv at night.
She watches a pride of pregnant tabbies stalk
cockroaches in the threadbare airport lounge
for protein enough to give a litter suck.
Always the Saving Remnant learns to scrounge
to stay alive. Could she now name the ten

plagues God sent? Uneasy truce exists
between these two antagonists.
El Al's flight, a frail umbilicus
that loops three times a week to the Holy Land,
is never posted on the Departures Board.
Security's intense. Shepherded
by an Israeli packing two guns,
she's bused with a poor handful to the tarmac.
The takeoff's dodgy, as if in fear of flak,

as if God might turn aside and harden
Pharoah's heart, again fill up the sea.
Once down, she knows the desert by its gardens,
the beachfront by its senior citizens
assembled for calisthenics on the sand.
An hour later in the Old City
she sees a dozen small white donkeys,
descendants of the one that Jesus straddled,
trot docilely beside Volkswagen Beetles,

Mercedes cabs, tour buses full of young
camera-strapped, light-metered Japanese.
She peers into archaeological digs that reach
down through limestone to the days of Babylon,
pridefully down to the first tribes of Jahweh
sacrificing scapegoats on a stone.
Down through the rubble of bones and matter
—Constantinian, Herodian, Hasmonean—
that holds up the contemporary clutter.

At the Western Wall, Sephardic Jews,
their genders separated by a grill,
clap for the bar mitzvah boy with spit curls
who struggles to lift a gold-encrusted Torah
that proclaims today he is a man.
The poet polkas, dancing to tambourine
and bongo drums with other passersby.
Behind her, dinosaurs against the sky,
two Hapag-Lloyd Ltd. cranes

raise massive stacks of facing stones,
the eighth or ninth or tenth civilization
to go up on the same fought-over bedrock.
Near the Via Dolorosa, among the schlock
for sale—amber beads, prayer rugs, camel saddles—
lamb legs are offered, always with one testicle
attached. Ubiquitous sweet figs, olive trees
botanically certified to be
sprouts from the sacred roots of Gethsemane.

She tries to haggle for a sheepskin coat
but lacks the swagger needed for cheerful insult.
A man whose concentration-camp tattoo
announces he was zero six nine eight
picks through a tangle of ripe kumquats
beside a Bedouin, her hands and face daubed blue,
who could as easily have been a Druid,

the poet thinks, and she an early Christian.
In a restored Burnt House from 70 A.D.,

the year the Romans sacked the second Temple,
she dutifully clambers down to view
scorch marks, gouged walls, some human bones, amid
a troop of new recruits in green fatigues.
Girls the shape and gawk of girls back home.
Boys whose bony wrists have overshot
their cuffs already. Not yet on alert
but destined to serve on one front or another,
eye contact in this shrine says: Jews together.

Meanwhile, clusters of Hasidic zealots
(most of them recent Brooklyn imports)
in bobbing dreadlocks and black stovepipe hats
pedal breakneck along the claustral streets
of the Arab Quarter on ten-speed bikes to await
the messianic moment any minute
now. Look for a pillar of fire and in it
the one true Blessed-be-He, whose very name
cannot be spoken in the waiting game.

The one true Blessed-be-He, who still is hidden.
The poet sees a film on television,
newsclips of shock troops: Syrian women
soldiers holding live snakes, biting them
on command, chewing and spitting out
the raw flesh. *In this way we will chew
and spit out the enemy.* Guess who.
Parental discretion was advised for viewing.
As if the young in these geographies

had not yet heard of torture, frag bombs, the crying
out at night that is silenced by garrote.
Another clip, the commentator said,
closeups of Assad's crack soldiers ordered

to strangle puppies and squeeze out blood
to drink as he reviewed the troops, was censored.
Judged too depraved for any audience.
How much is propaganda, how
much real? How did we get here,

the poet wonders, in the name of God,
in the name of all gods revving up their motors
to this high-pitched hum, like tripwire
stretched taut before the spark ignites the fuse
fragmenting life for life, blood running
in the dust to mingle Shiite, Druse,
Israeli, French, American.
If I forget thee, o Jerusalem,
may my right hand forget its cunning.

RUTH DAIGON

Refuge

As the body's laid out,
we stand at attention
waiting for the clearest light
and then sharpen our instruments.

First the eyes removed
to see what was seen,
ear probed to hear what was heard,
then the heart dissected
to find what was missed.

It takes time to cut tenderly
into the bone and sinew
of the past, each knife stroke
a loving incision.

There is no entrance.
Only entering.
And when the body's exposed,
we climb inside,
pull closed the flaps of skin
and slowly heal ourselves.

ED OCHESTER

Mary Mihalik

She'd tried to kill herself before.
Six kids, no money.

She was drunk
they said, doing 80, 90

on the slick blacktop
twisty and at dusk, and they

said there were no skidmarks
where she sailed under

the coal truck going slow
uphill out of the crossroad and

sheared the top of her Chevette
clean off and the rumor was

that when the cops came,
in the back seat they found her head.

People said all she needed
was a job, and I guess they're right.

And probably everyone thought
she needed love but everybody

says you've got to earn that,
though I think love's a gift,

the way money is for some, who
have a lot and never earned it.

I don't know. But a few nights later
when I walked past there, the insects

were at their cheerful static.
Aside from them the woods were silent.

And there were fireflies.

JUDSON MITCHAM

Loss of Power

The noon news chokes off, war in a man's throat.
The fan's blade quietly spins to a stop.
The bulb over a full sink fails. All this
happens at once, and a child shouts
"Hey" from the next room, comes
running to a man who is not surprised,
but oddly shocked, at the loss.

                             A mill worker,
a laid-off doffer in the card room who worked
sixteen hours routinely, he looks up
powerless to change this, and he thinks,
for the first time in his life, of the shape
the .38 would make in his pocket,
how no one would know him far away,
at a small bank in Ellijay
or a liquor store in Hartwell.

                            But tonight,
when his wife has laid out her tips on the steps,
far short of what Georgia Power wants,
he only walks, hands in his pockets, to the mill,
where he leans his forehead on the warm brick,
placing his palms on the trembling wall, feels
the power work through him like prayer.
For a long time, he stands like this.

R. T. SMITH

Shrine

Past the village
    the stream meanders
        and cuts stone slowly

with a saint's patience.
    And in fact, on a bend
        where the water skirts

a stand of willows,
    the rocks open
        into darkness, a grotto

where some peasant set
    a statue of St. Ambrose,
        and the farmers with

their women, their afflicted
    children have come for
        decades to hang medals

and holy cards, to light
    candles and pray toward
        the cave's deeper chambers

where the passage narrows
    and no man has ever
        been, but any visitor

in summer can see
    the quick dart of
        workers and hear

the multitude buzzing
    back in the shadows.
        Some imagine they can

smell the honey, and
    water from the shallows
        is sweeter by far.

Nearby flowers are
    abundant, and the rumor
        or superstition is,

of course, that God,
    a dark Madonna
        or at least the Ghost

        occupies the hive.

JUDITH KITCHEN

Solstice

for Nancy

Summers in Upstate New York
are not like your South, but you'll know
what I mean when I tell you days
simply deepened into a darker blue.
Evening stretched, hot
and lazy, as we slipped back out
to catch fireflies. On
and off, shooting stars.

Late November, each tree stark
in an old wind, nothing to see but headlights
tunneling the dark, the flat
sound of tires on pavement.
This is your question.
What if the earth did not swing back?
If we tipped on
into solid night, and cold?

In the vase, the papery hearts
of Japanese lanterns—orange against white.
If I knew answers, I'd tell you all
I know of death. But all I know
is second-hand, and pale.
Each night I count two sons sleeping
in the other room, a husband
to touch. And a need that nothing
satisfies. Here. I'll show you how
to walk in snow—toes first for the downhill,
heel in where the going's harder.

DOROTHY BARRESI

Pure Jesus, Early Morning Shift

Every cancer brings a bowl to clean.
Every operation has its mess.
Then who can afford even one
quick dream of the orderly on Psych
who's promised a beer with a blackout of kissing?
The only white girl in Sterilization
and Decontamination
nods off to a freight of bedpans
wheeled in, wheeled in.
Another laundry bag
stuffed with what's catchable
drops down the line.

The women shake their heads.
Facing off, they begin to sort
clamps and knives as if
not the giveaway tissue of the sick, but
a family secret were flushed down the drain.
And if summer doesn't kill them—
candyass college girls
the agency keeps sending—
if August doesn't put them once and for all
to its metal table,
they'll forget anger, forget
pluck it out.
The autoclaves whistle and sing to burn
morning from its blood.
Lunch is the only miracle.

NEAL BOWERS

The Rest

You can take it with you,
you know;
in fact you must—
the silence between words,
those moments of pure,
thoughtless reverie when sharpening
a pencil or stirring soup;
the pause between breaths;
the stop between diastole and systole
for which there is no name;
the space between the notes
without which the notes would be
one long wail.

Overhead, in the tall darkness,
a plane seems to circle,
its engine stopping and starting,
then stopping for good
as the farmer looks up from his mystery
and listens to nothing
punctuated finally by a distant thud.
In the morning he will stand
between rows of corn
before the wreckage so out of place
and small in his broad field,
as cameras click and whir
and someone reaches out a microphone
and waits for him to comment
on what he understands but can't explain.

MICHAEL McFEE

A Tumbleweed from Texas

When the world
is flat as West
Texas and the only
relief is the sight
of someone else's
accidental fortune
welling up and the sky
seems the merciless
iris of God, you
begin to understand
how regular people can
rob banks or execute
families out of plain
boredom, and why,
starved for motion,
this grown weed will
break itself off at
the ground and roll
away from its roots
until it becomes pure
economy of form,
refined by the sun
and wind into nothing
worth loving, a nomad
worshipping whatever
moves him and spills
his seed, a tinder-
hearted exile, a bush
ready for burning.

SUSAN LUDVIGSON

Burials

The difficulties of hiding anything.
How, for a child, it all seems easy.
I had a room behind my room,
a space back of the built-in drawers
next to the closet. I could
take a drawer out, crawl through,
and ease it back like a piece
in a puzzle. With a flashlight,
books, the world was as safe as Freiberg
before the war.
I kept my valuables there:
cigar boxes full of bottle caps
(worth money then—some kind of contest),
a pile of comics, the antique china doll
whose legs and arms I snapped one day
for spite.

Today I look through a notebook.
It has my name, but I know
none of this. Some of the words
I can't define, and books I discuss
I don't remember reading.
The writing is small and neat
like my aunt's. It almost draws pictures.

Sometimes even my face is a surprise.
I walk out happy, but someone comes up
on the street and asks what's wrong.
I think of last night's dream:

my father alive again at the table,
a baby crying, pages falling from the sky
like rain, and then like leaves
needing to be raked, put in order.
I can see which way the signs point,
but who would want to go there?

DABNEY STUART

Umpire

for my daughter

He learns to imagine
the vertical shaft of air
hanging above home, to hear
its inaudible hum
when pitches he can't see
tick its corners.
Under the lights, when
the humidity is right,
it becomes prismatic,
shimmering with the curve's kiss,
the slider's quick dive.
Sometimes, after calling
one perfect, pivoting,
driving his right arm out
and back in a groove smooth
as a piston's, he looks away

over the green swath toward
the lights, seeming to carry
that brightness in his eyes.
If he could hold it
there all
the time no one would
argue with him,
no distorted faces writhe
Hydralike into his, no benches
clear. Everyone would see

how his vision was the strike
zone—brilliant, impeccable,

fair. And the earth is flat,
and, next spring, bull-
frogs in Bradenton will
sprout wings. Still
he lets his mind wander
briefly inside that aura,
touching the certain borders
of his calling, his peaceful dream.

Then he edges back out of it,
watches the bright air disperse,
the pitcher lean in again
for his sign.
Crouching, he rests
his hand absently
on the catcher's ribs,
feels the tender
vibrations of the ball hitting
the mitt, sensing
the red seams' rapt
nestle into the leather.
It is, after all,

the dependable magic
instant he keeps waiting
on, between the ball's
untoward rest and his own
voice breaking the silence, before
he turns the invisible
quick trace of the pitch
into a statistic, building
the box score, the record
book, some other's dream.

JANE HOOGESTRAAT

Summer Darkness

Stepping that spring into southern rain with nothing
to protect the papers he carried rolled carelessly,
he paused, turning with a gaze beyond arrogance,
as though he meant to relinquish all caution, would
never seek shelter in a lighted doorway again
or speak another human word about danger.

Tonight fans rotate tediously, sirens announce
how late it has all become, the summer darkness
settles in, not less for coming later, breath
denser than winter and slower to arrive or leave,
and that face, voiceless, returns with a warning
from a corner in the mind that says only *swerve.*

ED ZAHNISER

Taking Stock of Feelings

Aches my left foot, arch already flat,
and gonads sag for lack of dalliance.
I crave support and wet warmth snug as a glove
yet tenuous, like a wide-brimmed hat
lodged against a windstorm's heady violence,
not to mention Love.

Nothing gives but what it gets
used up, worn out or failing that
contents itself to feed the universe
while guilt worries its spectrum like a rheostat
—or blows me skyward on jets.
I can't remember when, but I have felt worse.

Hostage monkhood's blindfolded silence, where has it gone?
Damnable thing, suspected, you can never hear it
pass like a quiver of empathy between captive and captor.
Birdsong clangorous squelches my spirit,
an exposed rabbit staring at a swooping raptor.
Sweet Christ, I'm flat out. It's only dawn.

CHARLIE SMITH

The Defiance of Heroes

In stories the old hero turns from the house
to linger in the courtyard
staring up long at the stars.
The scent of green wheat drifts from the fields,
tinged with the scent of the sea. In the stars
he sees the mouths of women and strong arms
raised. He can almost remember
what it felt like
to hold the golden bundle in his hands,
to raise it in the polished light
so high
the sun blazed brighter; and the stiff seas,
already legendary,
each wave an illuminated page
in his life's heraldry,
revealing another green island;
and the violence, free of rage
and lust—a pure, clear stream,
his whole body the stream.
It was like that.
Now in another kingdom
he sighs,
but not over loss, the fantastic adventuring.
Though goats bleating in the pen, the old stone house,
fields and contentious family are pitiful,
they do not matter. They do not matter.
Voyages end only
to reveal the ample treasure:

there is no home in this world.

MEMYE CURTIS TUCKER

Chipped Tooth

My tongue knows every inch of where it lives—
that animal, going round and round in its prison,
checking the stones.
It will worry this chip for days,
rubbing, pushing.
I throw in food, quiet it for a while,
then it begins to lumber around in the dark.
It wants things right, smooth, always the same.

There is nothing I can do, tongue,
for the tiny scar
that keeps you awake all day.
Everything grows old, has accidents—
someday, tongue,
even you.
Rest while you can,
warm in your cave.

JOE BOLTON

A Wreath of Stars: Symsonia, Kentucky, 1914

They'd caught me skimming cream off the top of the churn,
So half that winter I had to go upstairs
Right after supper without any dessert—
No comb-thick honey Mamie stored in jars,

No muscadine, no sunset-colored cake
Sweetened with molasses, no piecrust plumped
With apple or blackberry. Still, what made me ache
The most was missing that music my brother thumped

Out on his guitar while Pap's fiddle whined
Along like some hurt thing—like the bitch retriever
Hung up in barbed wire for hours, who tried
To eat me alive when I came to uncut her.

I'd climb those stairs like somebody going to heaven
Before he was ready, the loose boards creaking, then breathe
On my frosted-over window till seven
Cold stars shone on the dark sky in a wreath.

*

The night Pap and my brother didn't come in
For supper, Mamie told me to go ahead
And eat their peach cobbler. We waited, then—
I watching through my window while she read.

And along toward midnight I saw two figures weaving
Down the road: one tall and lean, the other

Much the same, singing and carefully passing
A thick glass jug between them—Pap and my brother.

They must have saved a month to buy that whiskey.
But leaning together, their sweet breath rising like clouds,
One passed the jug, the other didn't see,
And the glass broke open on the frozen ground.

They stared down at the spill as at a grave,
Then at each other—with hatred for a minute;
Then knelt down as though praying to be saved
And lapped up every star reflected in it.

BETTY ADCOCK

New South

For years I thought I still knew where
I was, that I was both there and here.
Home's what you take with you when you leave,
mean to or not. I thought some things were common
knowledge like those weeds you don't root out
since you can't anyway and might as well let be
what is as true as that. Like flaws in character
or the odd virtues that aren't explainable
but only common, and taken on in spite
of what you call them: wildflowers or weeds.

It's hard for me to say what's on my mind.
My life's been good, and for all sorts of reasons.
I'm glad for books and art. I've learned to like
good wine, and even learned, somewhat, to cook the dinner
that grows lighter and more difficult each year.
I saw the films, the ballet, raised a daughter
with all of what we used to call advantages.
I'm not liable to wear a foolish color
anymore, or some dumb thing in my hair.
And in some restaurants, you order salad later.

It's lovely where we live. Of course there aren't
grapevines or blackberry tangles. What is mostly
here is good taste, the natural-seeming
yards that cost so much to keep them seeming
natural. The city's nice enough and far enough
away. There don't seem to be graveyards.
No stone angels standing on the dead, ready

to take off but staying. Nobody
seems to *be* dead. Where are they?
They used to rise in stories a long time after.

It isn't that I don't like where I am.
I chose this place, with Tom. We're comfortable.
I love the things there are to know I never
could have known, once. My friends are smart
and talented. And I know them. In a way
they are myself, I think. There's an electric
kind of energy in them. I borrow that.
But it was like a shock, like waking up
in Belgium when you'd started out in Beaumont,
when I saw the quilts my friends had bought.

It's silly to be shocked. I don't know why
I was, or am. I know that quilts
are only artifacts like all the lost
things we enclose to look at in museums.
But these two, my two friends are so pleased:
a wedding ring and a ribbon quilt like a frame
of rainbows. I don't blame them. Well, certainly
I don't. The whole thing's silly. What
if they'll never know the makers. So what.
There was no reason I should feel so lost,

not knowing what to say. I thought of my own,
a dozen at least, not counting the ones
we sleep under, all folded in a chest
as old as they are. And each one with a name
and date pinned on. I don't know what
I thought. It isn't like me to be unable
to tell where I am standing, or if that is anywhere
on an ordinary afternoon. It was the second time
that week I'd seen a life hung up, not warming
anything in a houseful of glass and chrome.

I know I'm talking clichés, tacky nostalgia.
Everybody knows the past's not real.
And never was, somebody said. It's an idea
and you can change it, hang it up and make it
what you want or fear. Either way it's tamed.
One time I saw native Australian sand paintings
reduced to manageable size on canvas,
so we could see. It wasn't right, however beautiful.
Something they were meant for wasn't there:
the nature of things somehow. Like sand.

DEBORAH PIERCE NICKLAS

Daddy-long-legs

You appear from nowhere
dropped like a star
or urged from below like
some sea-creature.

At any rate, here
you're quite the critic
tapping the porch with
a leg repeatedly

at length continuing
smug, perfunctory—
all in little jerks
like an old movie.

Yet there's an antelope's
elegance about you
poised on the tips
of slender long legs

and a delicate order
as of a little loom
or fingers on a harp
or many knitting needles

as you nimbly set off
through the intricate grass
your plump pill body
aloft, sultan-style.

NANCE VAN WINCKEL

Somewhere: How Can We Leave It Now?

To keep ourselves from going anywhere
else, we tie ourselves
to something—and look out
across our landscape of beautiful debts

that goes on, far into the purple
stretches of space. Old
contradictions of chaparral and mesquite
line the long highways.

That belt of bets we made
against ourselves: to tough it out,
to fill our cellars with boxes and bottles.

The halter of habit, walking our little
dogs of love on their leather leashes.

The Indians say the road separates spirit
from spirit, deceives the meadowlarks
into devouring foxglove along the median strip.

Yet we admire the manacles of our big plans,
our tall words that go pale
then drift off into white graves.

The many handcuffs of busy signals
among the airwaves. The noose of November,
a stove stuffed with a bird,
cars full of guests at the door.

At the edge of it all the sea rocks forward
and back and whispers in its too-human voice,
that it could reach even us, sometime, somehow,
here in the middle of nowhere.

JUDITH ORTIZ COFER

La Tristeza

Books. By reading them,
by writing them, he thinks he has escaped
the sadness of his race.
When he returns to the old town,
open like a violated tomb, bleached bones
exposed to the sun, he walks bareheaded
among the people, to show his disdain
for the sombrero, the hat that humbles.
He has grown somber and pale
in the New England winter, ashamed
of the mahogany skin, the yellow teeth
of the men who move slow as iguanas
in the desert. When they greet him,
their eyes roll up to heaven, each claiming
to have been his father's most intimate friend.
Here they never let go of their dead.
And the women: timid blackbirds, lower
their eyes in his presence.
Damn the humility of the poor that keeps them
eating dust. He thinks this, even as he takes
the girl with skin supple as suede to his hotel
where her body spreading under him is a dark stain
on the clean white sheets he has earned.

DAVID R. SLAVITT

The Shadow

What boy has never envied Lamont Cranston,
invisible, able to fight for truth and justice,
defend his country, or slip unseen—and naked,
of course—into the girls' shower at school?
It isn't the trick we imagined but an art,
severe in its discipline, arduous (most of them are).

The limpid waterdrop, the rarefied
upper air, the even more abstract
refinements of science—radar or sonar—
betray nothing: this is the heart of the matter,
that knack of selflessness, the purity
of attention that never refracts, never reflects.

You see, or don't, the perfectly clear pane
in shop windows. They curve, disappear, tempting
the not-so-innocent passerby to suppose
he might reach out to scoop up a quick handful
of gold and gems. That appetite for riches
is what the illusion is likely to kindle. The real

abnegation of crystal—if only the ball
were perfect, we couldn't see it at all, and the gypsy
might yet peer into the future's maw—
sets the impossible standard of refinement
I know enough now only to dream of:
to sneak into that school shower, to see

with neither lust's reflection nor sentiment's
refraction those girls' young bodies and as clearly
their lives and deaths—as Dr. Chekhov might,
or angels were they to eavesdrop on their giggles.
I have held my breath so to listen
to a brook's faint purl I thought I'd imagined

but couldn't imagine where. All of us know
what evil lurks in the hearts of men. What's harder
is what is good and unremarkable
except to the gazing eye, flawless, selfless
as that glass, air, water. Obtuse, opaque,
The Shadow got it wrong, knew nothing at all.

NANCY SIMPSON

Grass

We ought to be thankful it grows wild
on roadbanks, sometimes blond and curled.
It holds earth together and still
we hear Earth is falling.

Sink holes in the south swallow cars.
We do not doubt, but can we help wonder
what happens when the bottom drops?
Maybe clumps fall with the Jeep

and the Porsche, forming the shoreline
of a lake, in some posh suburb.
Grass has a right to be cherished,
Crowning Glory, clipped to perfection.

No matter where we sleep we live
with threat hanging over our lawns.
Who says we need more weapons?
We want to know what will happen to grass,

grass everywhere, amber savannahs,
sacred as the hair on our heads.

EDWARD WILSON

For the Woman in Her Station Wagon Weeping at a Red Light

It's like watching the dead
winter yard through the window above
the radiator, the glass itself
rippling almost. Or this street
the August sun has slapped
hour after hour until parking meters
are a line of woozy drunks
and even the brick stores billow
like sheets on the line.

You have been carrying it all day,
a glass impossibly full,
and didn't know until this wavering
of everything spilled over.

And not because you are unhappy.
You've lived long enough to know
that love comes home exhausted
and falls asleep on the couch
with his shoes on.

The tune on the radio, the limping boy—
whatever's jogged your elbow
isn't dramatic, unbearable. It's
hardly even yours yet, though if
you thrashed among the leaves like towhees
in the woodlot there would be something
in that sweet rot to seize on.

Meantime, there is no shame
in crying while the light is red.
You live in a rich country.
You have tears to spend.

BILLY COLLINS

Last Sunday in October

Tonight is the night we turn back the clocks
as if the globe were a combination lock
and we could move all the time zones one click west.

We rewind time to the beginning of an hour
and relive it, like a trick in science fiction
or a second take in the making of our film biographies.

But the hour is still fresh, not redundant or even familiar.
The dog moves his weight from the couch to a corner.
Tea cools in a blue cup, and the wind stiffens
and turns to face a more wintry direction.

Is this the same hour we lost in spring,
the one parents used to promise we would get back,
returning to us now colder and heavier by months,

full of early dawns sparkling in farmhouse windows
and afternoons when children carry their games
through the softening gray light and into the dark?

TED KOOSER

Spider Eggs

In the shadows under the cellar stairs,
the fear of darkness, spinning there
all day with the steady whirr
of an old refrigerator, has formed
a solar system all its own:
five pea-sized planets, slung in a web
of dust and frozen propane gas,
orbit the spark in a spider's skull—
too dense a head to let the light out
onto the clouds of dirty laundry—
but bright in its own black way
and pulling all the light in after it,
one fifty-watt bulb at a time.

JAMES APPLEWHITE

Tree of Babel

Fair day, your green air
Freshened from bodies of cedar
And holly. The river's metal
Reflection shone molten.
Rocks washed of silt
Left the mind rinsed.
The hank of cloth in a fork
Like a scrap tacked to fact
From dream was gone.
On the shore crossed to by cable,
I looked back at the people
Hiking on Sunday.
I waved before fading
Into trees. The boot print
I found in a clearing
(Like Friday coming on Crusoe)
Stunned me. A hundred yards on,
An ancient, forked beech
Etched by illegible scars
Of letters seemed text
To the living story
Of abandoned rows under trees.
A scribble of vines loaded
My head like a dictionary's
Waste heap.
Ice spike sycamore
Beyond the written beech,
You spired air
With absolute moment.

I discovered the illusion
Newly. Perception's pool
Inked only by branches,
You are garden before
Transgression, flood high over
The Babel tower. I came
Home from this year
Made new with only a happy
Headache, a thorn in my finger.

PETER MEINKE

Sonnets for a Diabetic

Sentimentalist, you loved words like *doom*
and felt it stalking you through foreign halls;
but at the end they found you in your home,
unromantic, in that familiar room
alone, forgetful: insulin withdrawal.
In your back pocket some pills, keys, the comb
you seldom used, and an unfinished poem—
you never finished poems. Instead, you'd call,
late at night, one by one your sleeping friends,
reciting in that Appalachian drawl
your wonderful one-liners, like a groom
wooing his bride with shining bits and ends
of jewelry before the night descends.
My life, you said: *Lies taut upon the loom.*

In your rich brain the end must have burned better
even while crawling toward the phone you loved:
some images, exotic from your trips,
some grand betrayal, some unanswered letter
had brought you to your knees in pools of blood,
and you blew out with poetry on your lips.
I hope so. Old friend, to see you slip
away without a scene! Today, I rubbed
my eyes and half expected you to rise
and look around, pull on your thin gray gloves,
stride out into our stricken winter weather
and, waving at the birds, to shout: *Surprise!*
But nothing happened. Again I rub my eyes:
I see the last time that we drank together.

We sat beneath the jacaranda tree
catching the purple petals in our beer,
a royal carpet soft under our feet—
that was *your* effect: anyone could see
this was just another dingy bar, too near
the traffic to be comfortable, the heat
not helped much by the scraggly tree, and Pete
the bartender surly, cheap, and mean. Here,
once more, you spoke your lines—just last July!—
it was your way of publishing: "No mere
book that no one reads, or needs, but a free
voice to a friend who won't forget." And I
remember: *All day long the day goes by.*
A lovely line. A gift from you to me.

And all day long the day goes by. Your line
echoes through my aching head today
(we'd drink to *wretched excess,* so when
I heard the news, I did again). Through wine
we tried to speak the truth, each in his way—
but you were better. I held back, and then
you chided me: "Confess! Confess! All men
are sinners!" You loved high drama, the play
of tragic forces you claimed had passed you by.
This was never true. Your life went the way
you aimed it: nowhere, slowly; now mine
seems coarser, I confess. *I confess!* In the sky
a plump mourning dove hoots its baleful cry,
useless perhaps, and yet how free, how fine.

BETTIE SELLERS

There Was a Place We Could Have Met

Russian astronauts
are returning to earth
having failed to dock
with their space lab
somewhere just west
of the ninth star
beyond Betelgeuse.
That must have been
where it was—
in space so vast
my mind can only fantasize
a neighborhood with Castor
on one corner, Pollux waiting
at another, missing his brother
as you failed to find me
standing so long
at the bus stop
on the square in St. Remy.

MARK DOTY

It Begins

       with a fragment of conversation
you probably misunderstood, a blurred remark
that perhaps didn't refer to you. Or were you sleeping?
Then it's something in the way the distant,
familiar skyline is arranged this morning,
a steeliness in the click of your new shoes
you hadn't noticed, something in the click
of the taxi door, even the short black hairs
on the back of the driver's neck seem to be clicking.
It's the kind of day your sentimental mother
would have said the clouds carried baskets
of fresh laundry, or the angels were waxing
the floors of heaven blue. You'd have laughed,
but by noon you wouldn't be surprised
if the clouds rained wet sheets, or huge knees
bruised the upper atmosphere. It's as if
you have aluminum foil on your fillings,
you tell the office manager, and by three
you're home, leaning into the gilt zero
of the bathroom mirror, watching for signs
in that changeable forecast, your face,
bending into the noose of white, advancing weather.

ALBERT GOLDBARTH

Off

One night in a bar a voice
not even Scotch can smooth the
longing from cries "God

I want to die!" and when I look
at everybody looking I see it's
my voice. I've been there this

long: the flowers outside,
like an ancient regent's liveried retainers
and spangled wives, have followed the

solar rise and fall—now
that he's set, I know from reading,
they'll throw themselves in the grave

as well. I explain this Neolithic custom
to a guy above a Bud, and just
as for no apparent reason my detailing

Mesopotamian funerary figures makes
me weep like a child, he interrupts
as if he hasn't heard a single word

about the chalcedony-work, and says
the day his woman left with some
fuck who serviced a candy and coke machine

route, he also heard he'd lost it
all in the scheme to open a waterbed

market in Paraguay. "Every goddam

penny. There weren't no waterbeds anywhere
there, it was perfect. Ha,
perfect!" This guy's a little

off. The woman next to him's off by
about a country mile—with the gestures
of a captain rushing the last of the passengers

into the last of the lifeboats, she's
recounting her honeymoon, something to do
with the Peapatch Motel and a parrot

on the showerstall—"really." So much is
off, misunderstood, and dazzlingly infirm,
so much is sudden epic schizophrenic

word-salad in a hearing trumpet, I
toast it, toast whatever's missed
the target by a nick, so discovered

the loveliness of the tangent: Einstein
flunking high school math, that accidental
pour of the pot on the stove that melted

into the first industrial rubber, every star
that isn't in a constellation but burns
on the side in its black sconce none the less,

so many stars! It must be
some shade of morning in Paraguay. It's
the pit of things, here. I've been in it this

long: I don't want to die. These flowers
follow the sun through heaven, sure, but
don't give up holding to Earth for one second.

P. C. BOWMAN

Helen Approaching

And these, as they saw Helen along the tower approaching,
Murmuring softly to each other uttered their winged words.
　　　—Iliad, III, 154–155.

Helen standing on the city wall, composed as the clouds,
Light and ambiguous as these, still supple in old men's eyes,
Filled to the brim their vision till Panthoos asked aloud
If she were not the sort of blessing one might call mixed.

At length Antenor answered, "The gods are full of tricks,
And give with one hand what they take back with the other.
The balance of our life is thus forever fixed
On zero," and he coughed into his tired hand.

The group fell silent, but Thymoites' sly eyes scanned
Each wrinkled face. "The wise man holds the reins,
Perhaps, but stallions pull the weight. As he understands
Zeus' ways so well, perhaps Antenor might undertake

To remember his own, when he was Paris' age. The young rake,
Like a lovesick bull, pursued Theano through Troy's streets,
And when she first refused him, threatened to find a lake
Proper for such grief, and drown himself in it."

At that the wise men laughed, and recalled the adolescent
Each once had been, and so Helen found them by the gate,
Their voices smooth and sweet as wine with honey in it:
Their eyes gazed through her as if they gazed on clouds.

ERIC TRETHEWEY

Garbage

We hauled trash that summer, the three of us,
an old man, a hard young man, and a boy.
Morning by afternoon there were runs
to Whitzman Bros. scrap metal yard
and to the dump on the outskirts of town.
The job was at Poole's garage, cleaning out
a junkyard in the vacant lot next door.
The junk had to be sorted piece by piece,
salvage to one corner, the rest on the truck.
Mornings were for the metal, heavy stuff first.
We winched up motors, bulldogged transmissions
and rear axles, bowled rims from across the lot.
When the truck was half-full of iron and steel,
we would top off the load with rusty tin—
doors, trunk-covers, stove-in hoods and fenders—
and haul it all away to the scales.

Afternoons, we loaded up with garbage
the boss knew no one would ever pay to have:
rotten furniture, old bones, clutch-plates, rags.
Then, smeared with dirt, three-deep in the cab,
we would drive it away to the water's edge
where roaring dozers butted the mounded trash,
and rancid smoke coiled out of the debris.
After the first few trips it was no surprise
to see him, a skinny black man in a peaked cap,
waiting to back us around to the edge
and watch with care our careless tossing off.
He and his partners sifted each load

for something of value we had missed.
They set aside mud-filled bottles for refunds
and wire that promised copper under the grease.
Broken boards they saved for winter fires
in windy shacks at the edge of the dump.

Their field office crowned a hill of junk.
Held up by two-by-fours and a door frame,
a rotten canvas canopy sagged above
old car seats and a disemboweled chair
where they dogged it when business was slow.
An ancient ice-box squatted to one side,
and from the door-frame hung a cowbell, clapperless.
Their look-out beat it with a tire-iron
when the police cruiser nosed into view.

The man sold bootleg liquor on the side.
On the day's last trip, and sometimes its first,
Granddad and Stu would buy a pint from him,
offer him a swallow and stand around his lean-to
drinking and yarning in the sunny stench.
They'd forget about Poole, his ninety cents an hour,
the black wind drifting low over the burning,
and I, just a boy then, would watch them,
listen carefully, begin to learn how it was
a man could live like this if he had to.

KATHRYN STRIPLING BYER

Jericho's

walls shone not half so bright
under Jehovah's moon as he sees this mountain
stand to the west of his idle fields,
daring him climb it for what
reason he's never told me straight
out, though I know he dreams deer

by the multitude wander
my sleepless nights, safe within Jericho's
unexplored shadows he tells me not even the Cherokee
ever tracked. When he gets hungry
for wild meat, he disappears,
firing a parting shot into the chicken coop.

Soon enough he brings the same story
home to my empty pot, how he was led
by a golden buck, into the clouds
where it bolted clear over the edge of the world
and he found himself suddenly light
headed, cursing his luck and the creatures

that roam as he would, with no reason
to turn back the way he had struggled
up, clinging to rocks
breaking loose from his hold on what
little by little comes
tumbling down into the valley.

RON SMITH

Running Again in Hollywood Cemetery

December: Richmond, Virginia

Nothing's changed here
since you and I climbed the sagging
chain link and honeysuckle
off Cherry St. to sprint the steep hills
of the dead. We knew what we wanted:
granite thighs for trampling linemen,
legs that could launch us over the caged faces
to break the plane between us
and gold figures we envisioned marching
across our mantels; women whose red lips
glistened and parted for everything
we could give them.

Coach ordered hills
so we ran here in a pumping race to this crest
where we stomped two presidents
with our breakdown drills,
where this stained woman still bends
a face I will never see into her metal hands.
Neither falling behind, we took each other
on a tour of lies, past the white slab
where you laid Sandy and showed your ass
to a screaming widow who lashed you bloody
with a dozen roses while you by God
went on and finished,

past the filth-eyed angels
drooping with sorrow, shrouded obelisks

and artfully broken columns,
sandstone tree trunks carved intricate
with rot, the gothic Randolph tomb
where I crowbarred the bronze
one August afternoon on Laura's dare,
where the west window broke the darkness
into colors over her shivers, and she laid back,
the Virgin's blue cloak across her scar
and my chest war painted,

and she said, I'm safe,
and I didn't believe her and spilled my seed
in Randolph's deep-carved name.
Which were the lies? Was the heavy door
already open? Did I really pour myself
into that gray stone? In the locker room your skinny ass
never had a scratch that I remember.
And what do we have now? Your Saturday
headlines have shrunk to one small name
in black marble not far from Lincoln's huge,
tired eyes in that other capital we cursed
with our simple history.

Alone in Vermont ice
I've tried to chase it all down,
pound some sense into it, like the time
I bloodied knuckles on Jeff Davis' cold jaw
and then on you because you thought
my whiskey meanness was Yankee sacrilege.
In the blinding light at breakfast we blamed
our bloody shirts and fist-changed faces
on the Church Hill boys.

Since then I've run
more miles than you ever ventured from home,
even for that jungle assault when
you came up vapor just before
your first R&R. They went back and back

for a week after pushing past that blasted clearing.
Nothing, not a dog tag, not a silver filling.
In the only letter you ever finished
you wrote of another city you never laid eyes on,
dreamed of yellow-faced women waiting
to set you on fire with
American diseases.

Today, lean for distance,
I have circled all the unchanging dead
with only a little chest burn, chasing
my breath up and down every hill I could find.
The pencil-necked guard who scared us away
in '65 is white-headed now, and almost fat.
He still chains the gate at sundown.
As early gold takes the Confederate pyramid
and every plinth and angel, a couple, arm in arm,
is walking on the flaming river far below.
I turn back for the granite arch
while there is still time.

JODY BOLZ

Bonsai

Two centuries to keep a maple
three hands high.
The Japanese are patient people.

Why not master me, keep me
from jungling up the world, beguile
me, hold my heart still
in one small garden?

Another stratagem.
Summer kimono with landscape:
ten embroidered deer,
wisteria and pines.
Not a cloud in the lake.
No guesthouse.
You stop by to see the grounds.
Please don't bother—please—
I can't rake the paths each week
and tie the cats
over-tending children we don't have.
I make mistakes.

Bird songs in our room,
a record,
aren't the woods.
Not even an aviary.
You get dizzy on them anyway—

imagining they're real,
the bonsai is a wild tree,
tiny dish its island,
yard its sea,
all your art your life
and your love safe.

FRED CHAPPELL

Forever Mountain

(*J. T. Chappell: 1912–1978*)

Beyond the curl of scrub pine hills,
Beyond the Pisgah-eating Rat, behind
The grisaille of new-leaved hickory ridges,
Past Black Gap opening its vistas like a chinoise fan,
There is a deeper mist of mountains.
                              Unseen till now.
The tumbled mezzotint range unknown because
The weather was too close.

But now a marble smoke has cleansed my vision.

I see my father has gone to climb
Easily those slopes, taking the time
He's got plenty of, making good headway
In the fresh green mornings, stretching out
Noontimes in the groves of dogwood and oak.
He has found a walking stick of second-growth hickory
And through the amber afternoon he measures
Its shadow on the flank of the mountain.
    Not marking the hour, but seeing
The quality of light come over him.
He is alone, except what voices out of time
Come to his head like bees to the beetree crown,
The voices of former life now indistinct as heat.

By the clear trout pool he builds his fire at twilight,
And in the night a granary of stars

Rises in the water and spreads from edge to edge.
He sleeps, to dream the simple dream
Of the horses of pine trees, their shoulders
Twisting like silk in the high wind.

He rises early-glad and goes his way,
Taking piecemeal the mountain that possesses him.

My eye blurs with blue distance, I see no more.
Forever Mountain has become a cloud
Which light confuses and murmured songs dislimn.

    This is a prayer.

B. D. LOVE

Carp

He pulls through the shallows,
Thick, garnet-finned, languid
Though quick to start, leaving a tuft
Of silt where he has been, a silt trail
Hanging in the water a long while,
Like smoke from a dump fire.
He won't go far. He likes his time.
He likes what other fish shun.
No vice-jawed killer like the pike—
No bass, either, no mass of muscle
Scaled emerald, silver, obsidian,
He's a danger only when hit:
That bulk—and he can grow to twenty,
Thirty pounds—can sheer a pin
And make a motor whir, at worst.
He is all slow, overgrown goldfish,
The scales more brass than gold
And crusted with a green like verdigris.

Unlike those others, say the bass
Who bolts into the air, jerking
Like a sprung trap to toss a hook,
Or the pike, cunning in shadow,
Who springs quick as a stiletto,
He will not strike. He sucks.
He draws up. He caresses
With that fleshy mouth that scares
Some boys—obscene the undulation
As he gulps the air, profuse the blood,

Real blood, dense red, that flows
When a hook is gouged out.
The feelers, some say, cut, but don't.
Another tale has rubies set
Inside, behind each ear.

But Carp is of the flesh:
Bottom eater. Trash fish. Scavenger.
Though easy—and legal—to take
With a .22, bow and arrow, spear, snag-hook,
A baseball bat, though a small one
Logs five pounds and doubles rods,
Makes reels wheeze and the young heart
Pound before he's recognized,
He is not kept. He will not serve
As fertilizer, even, somehow
Wrenching himself back above ground
Where he will flop for hours,
Untouched by dog or cat.

Perhaps you have walked along
An old canal or dying river
Heavy with topsoil the instate land
Lost not so much to water as to greed,
To overgrazers. You may have
Watched for rings on the surface,
Where at twilight fish once kissed
The rim of the world and drew back
Water striders, wriggling larvae,
And flies. Your water gone, what's left
Gives back a muddy azure, like
A mildewed mirror. Kick at stones.
Watch for him. He's moving there,
Among the browned-out lilies,
The rotting roots. At first
You won't make out the shape—
Covered, as he is, by a silt

As thick as time. This mobile bog
Is Carp, feeling his way along,
The great tail stirring dirt
Which falls across him, falls
Like a mantle, richly brown.
He seems familiar, the image
Of some sage, or like those men
Who have no names, no homes,
Who pull along your city's streets,
Who burn oily rags in garbage cans
For heat at night,
Who smell.

Carp goes on.
Carp will endure the dark water,
Though it kills all else.
Go on, he says. *I am trash, am bottom.*
Go cast for your glimmering rippers,
Your swallowers whole.
I take what's left.
I will make you no good eating.

4

The 1990s

Prozac, 1987. In 1993, the seminal book *Listening to Prozac* by Peter Kramer, a practicing psychiatrist, questioned the ethics of altering personality through this new type of drug, which he acknowledged as effective and transformative. In the 1990s millions of Americans took some form of antidepressant. Probably no connection here, but many mainline religious denominations experienced significant decreases in their congregations. Pope John Paul II, however, did manage to lift the Inquisition edict (1633) against Galileo Galilei. New Age spiritual approaches took hold. In *Southern Poetry Review* during this era, healing trumped any other theme. Facing the end of the second millennium, the country had major jitters.

Not many people really believed the world would end at midnight 1999, did they? More rigorous souls reminded everyone that the third millennium did not begin officially, anyway, until the end of the year 2000. But what about computers? Y2K might spell doomsday if all the world's computers crashed because they could not convert to "2000." And more and more, we depended on computer technology. The World Wide Web, the Internet, search engines, e-commerce, email, all promised to connect everyone, to reinforce the new sense of "global community." Violent protests against the World Trade Organization meetings at the end of the decade called into question the coziness of that phrase. The stock market soared to new highs during the 1990s but headed for a crash, one brought about largely by the dot-com bubble and what chairman Alan Greenspan of the Federal Reserve Board called "irrational exuberance" on the part of investors. Was everyone taking too much Prozac, banking too much on technology?

Twenty-four-hour CNN coverage now made it seem that the world never slept, and as usual most news tended to the bad. Had so many serial killers always walked among us? The Columbine shootings and others that followed introduced us to the darkest side of Generation Y. What it meant to be human came under further scrutiny with the advent of controversial cloning. Timothy McVeigh, the Unabomber, bin Laden, Saddam Hussein. For most of the decade, Iraq played at disarmament with the U.N. The Gulf War, the Third Balkan War, Kosovo. The World Trade Center bombing in 1993; U. S. embassy bombings in 1998. The world was loud with detonations, real and imagined. Terrorism at home and abroad would become the national anxiety.

However, not every poem in the journal during this decade had fingernails bitten to the quick. One finds moments of indelible healing, as in Peter Makuck's "After" and Neal Bowers's "A Legacy," as well as ironic, funny takes on the theme, as in Kathy Evans's "Psychic Healers" and Starkey Flythe Jr.'s "Paying the Anesthesiologist." Though not the only subject matter during this era, its persistence suggests a gravitational pull on the editors. *Southern Poetry Review* passed from Robert Grey to Ken McLaurin and Grey's wife, Lucinda, in 1991. In 1994, McLaurin assumed editorship and held the post until the journal moved to Savannah, Georgia, in 2002. Oddly enough, one reason for his retirement from the position involved the issue of health.

"Against Healing" by Paul Allen opens this section. It is a poem adamantly about spiritual healing, but one set against any sort of quick fix or the worst of New Age "newage" (the "s" replaced). It also rejects conventional Christianity with a memorable, opening phrase: "Original sin, my ass." Rather, the poem's epigraph, a sentence from a letter by Rilke, provides the poem's compass: "Whoever lets go in his fall dives into the source and is healed." That sense of slow motion freefall prevails in "American Insomnia" by Gwen Ebert, which concludes this section, a poem asserting that the whole country craves profound rest, but it cannot turn "off" everything that stays "on" all the time. Its technology and materialism madden and enslave. The poem's hellish premise is not that we do not choose to slow the pace, or to stop, but that we cannot choose to do either one. The ambiguous "it" in the poem is not exactly a runaway train, but "It's on 24 hours a day, tireless as a glacier."

PAUL ALLEN

Against Healing

Whoever lets go in his fall dives into the source and is healed.
                    —Rainer Maria Rilke

Original sin, my ass. In the beginning the earth was
whatever darkness was, and wet—was Rhonda's
mother down at the end of the road
who took me to her bed, that stuff you've read
about—Chopin on the record player,
Orpheus holding a vase across the room.
The birds and the bees loved her leaves,
her wild world of shadows around that house.
Me and my Red Ryder pump, rolling
my tongue to feed the gun with BBs,
ammunition from my mouth.
I got good. But when she'd call me in
to her, I was bad. I would come for more
than killing birds and bees. I would come
to be found out there, to be brought in
for music, wine, to feel her hand on mine,
hear the shot roll down the magazine
when she disarmed me at the door.
I learned a lot on her property.
But her music never demented me
like my own loves did or songs
in honky-tonks, roadside taverns serving
hope with a twist while the sun came up
in brush strokes on painted panes in the john.
Enough of that, you get to know the peace
sad arms can bring when what's-their-names

take money or the meal or the ride to town
up front. Among such as these, you teach yourself
a new language, learn to pun to see how far
you can push words to make a proposition
clear—to seal a deal without being slapped
in jail. But even before you got that sick
you learned to peek, then look. Then take:
titties on the Tasadai, the dugs at Bergen Belsen,
public showers, flowers on the surfer's pouchy trunks
(or trunky pouch), the smell of a her or him
on the phone in the park that stays on
the side of your head to the river porno shop
with all its sneaking, starving least of these
where you begin to believe you belong.
By the time you feel the need to heal,
your standards are shot to hell.
You wouldn't know *well* if you could custom order it.
Try it. Go back to that Motel 6 again. Check in,
stand naked as the day you were born.
There in your garment of animal skin:
epidermal, hirsute, infested
with the stuff of documentaries:
examine yourself in the streaked mirror
with an eye to love: hair all over's going,
or growing scattered, skin's cracking, stretching
over your swelling joints, veins bursting
into bright pattern: You're molting, Pale Scales.
You're no ordinary, garden variety man: You're
serpentizing. I'm not sure you'd want to heal
before you had witnessed that. I'm not too sure you can.

CATHY SMITH BOWERS

Paleolithic

We love these old caves—Lascaux,
Altamira—and walk carefully
the way we always enter the past,
our hands bearing
the artificial light of this world.

We imagine those first hunters
crouched, conjuring luck,
carving into rock-swell
their simple art—whole herds of bison,
the haunches, the powerful heads, floating
orderless along the walls.
And some are climbing sky
as if they were stars, planets
orbiting something they cannot see.
Centuries will pass before they
right themselves, their hooves
coming down onto the deep
wet floor of leaf-fall.
Remembering earth.
Remembering where it was
they were headed.

DAVID AXELROD

Georgic: For My Friends Who Never Find Any

Like the universe, that's how wild mushrooms
grow from forest mold: everywhere

is the center, find one erect pileus
and spiral outward in concentric rings.

In this way you'll pick all you need
to fill your bucket with black morels

any morning in May, when heart-leaf arnica
covers the forest floor in unbroken green

that ripples like pond water, whenever wind
tires of the pinetops and comes down

to search among modest things
closer to ground. I tell you this because

you'll have to kneel down a great deal,
pray to the mountain's god, who may answer,

booming overhead or pelting you with sleet and hail.
You'll have to get on your knees, peer under

the green shadow of arnica—canopy nearest earth,
someone else's heaven, green sky of a world

always underfoot, trampled, ignored,
very much like the other world you know better.

But here, you visit only during a few weeks
each spring, your giant face reappearing

like a rare planet returned from its eccentric orbit.
Which means you spiral, too, your life

another ring in a pattern of rings with a random
center of gravity. Or there is no gravity

and you are one among many wanderers
wobbling blind through space, until

that metaphor evaporates like sleet and hail
melting back into sun-lit air, and you're just

standing here at the edge of a dark grove
of Douglas firs that didn't fall to a chainsaw,

and right here at the margin between
what was destroyed and what was not,

you clap your hands, laugh, and quickly kneel.

SIMEON BERRY

Los Alamos

> *We're all sons of bitches now.*
> —Bainbridge to Oppenheimer at zero plus one minute

We called it the Dragon, they called it
Project Omega, though it came down
to Slotin checking the potency of the bomb
fragments. He poked them together
with a screwdriver until the Geiger counter
ticked like the metronome in the cockroach's
antennae and he could read the runes
shaped in that ruined puzzle.
He worked months before he slipped:
they gave off a blue glow and the other six
knew they might be dead in that instant,
but not know it, might go back
to their wives in their clean coats
but with the symbols they'd created
twisting the chalk in their bones
and rewriting the red spirals in their veins.
Slotin knew, and Graves, who had stood
with his hand on Slotin's shoulder
as if he were already staring
into the cataracts, but they called
Graves's wife to calculate his chances.
She punched in equations until someone
told her it was her husband. But Slotin
knew he had looked too deep
into the unlight while the radiation sunk
pure uninflected arrows into him.

He knew the chaos that instantly bred,
the parts erased from the atom's
glazed circle. Subtracted from space,
he was raised, incorruptible
in the knowledge of his own end.
And he was the one, lunging across the desk
toward that scattered square,
who shut the box with his own body.

PHEBE DAVIDSON

It seems to her now

that her life has always
been full of the voices
of other people. Her grandmother
naming the early springs—

> *anemone, hepatica,*
> *blood root—*

the dogtooth violets
they would dig up and bring
back to the yard,
her mother reading

> *Christopher Robin*
> *is saying his prayers,*

& singing one sad, silly
tune from her college years,
her father's voice
pitched low

> *Lights out now,*
> *sweet dreams—*

as if sweet dreams
could save her from the scent
of violets making her weep,
from her mother screaming

> *Get away.*
> *Get away from me.*
> *I know what you've done—*

from one friend dying,
another dead, from the voice
of a third who fills the air

with inflection and concern,
each syllable

>   *Lights out now,*
>   *sweet dreams—*

from this knowing
without knowing how to say it
that what she needs is silence,
that she cannot bear to hear
another word.

PETER MAKUCK

After

In the low afternoon light,
a long row of cottonwoods led us out of Santa Cruz,
a small cemetery off in the desert.

That day, a few days before Christmas,
your father in front beside me, I kept seeing
the seat beside you empty,

and him, as I drove, stare through
the passing mesquite to some other place perhaps,
silence enforcing a distance.

Lame, he had held my arm,
looked down at the unhealed turf, then crossed himself,
thin shoulders quaking. I looked

beyond the wall, across
the creosote flats, and watched a coyote drag something
limp toward a culvert.

Back in the car, I kept seeing,
tethered to stones, all those mylar balloons—"Feliz Navidad"
or "Te quiero" in the shape of a heart—

emblems of another culture,
telling us how far from home we were, the balloons
tormented in the desert wind.

Before houses again rose up

and the gaudy lights of Phoenix hid an endless sky
where stars began to glimmer,

we stopped at a traffic light,
emptiness everywhere but this rancho of cracked adobe,
chickens and a single goat.

In front of the corral,
a Mexican sat on a kitchen chair, his face tipped back
and bronzed like a mask.

We watched a young woman
trim his hair, then lean down for a whisper and a kiss,
their faces wrinkled with laughter,

making me ease the car ahead
to center and frame them in the open gate at our side,
while we waited for the light.

Your father turned
and watched them too, and though his face was shadowed,
I saw his features tighten and focus.

After the woman ran her fingers
through her husband's long dark hair and trimmed again,
your father closed his eyes and smiled.

Their voices came inside
but they never looked our way as we watched, oblivious
as a family photo

finished by a boy in a red bandanna
entering from the right, chasing a black chicken
and making it fly.

Before we left that crossroads
with whatever it was we needed, the light went green
two or three times, I think.

MARGARET HOLLEY

Living Mysteries

Father raised pigs for ham and bacon,
the sow so fat with young
she lay like a seed pod ready to burst.
We held the piglets in our arms like infants,
all belly and tiny limbs.

Growing out of myself into another age
I walked through the fire of the hayfield
toward the darkness of the barn,
taking forever. I walked through decades,
still surrounded by flames,

a ripening body of vast inner distances,
fifty thousand miles of vessels and capillaries,
each month a new moon, a new outer layer of skin.
When we sat down to dinner,
grandfather carved the glistening roast,

windows open, no one watching but us,
still eating the old gods,
the autumn air pregnant with future,
already thick with rumor—
destruction of the sanctuary at Eleusis in 400 A.D.,

its mysteries safe
in the everyday clothing of holiness:
unobserved acts of kindness, healing of wounds,
and slowly down its tendrils
spirit descending into the river of blood.

DEBORAH POPE

Mammogram

I made the mistake
of looking down—
breast coaxed away
from my chest to end
in a thinned-out puddle
of tissue, between plastic
clear as a grade-school petri dish,
some specimen pithed and opened,
suspended for view in a jar,
and all those playground
taunts come true,
flat, in fact,
as a pancake.

But the film clipped up later
in the doctor's light
transformed the world,
like the first satellite reports
of a visionary landscape,
celestial, sublunary,
nicked with grainy brilliance,
a curved, primitive planet
I floated, tethered,
proprietary, above.

Then *there* and *there*,
his offhand ballpoint
tapped like a miner
at the marvelous crust,

gauging the find,
the wedge of entry,
and I turned back
from the black and white
prospects of that surface
to the featureless scape
drawn out by machine,
saw it for what it might
easier, better, have been—
a cheek fast under ice,
or a face, hard
against a windshield.

CHARLES HARPER WEBB

The Weight of Knowledge

You barely feel it, light as the first hairs
on your bald head: "Ma-ma," "Da-Da," "Poo-poo."
Every week brings more: name, age, birthday,
control of body-functions, the magic of "No!"

Facts cling to you, sticky-sweet as jujubes:
the laws of grammar and balancing on two feet;
the way a stone feels, how to throw it,
what it does to a glass tray.

Learning grasps your bones and pulls:
I before *e* except after *c*. Three times three
is nine. Field grounders on the short hop.
If teenagers yell "Hey kid!" at you, run.

Information pumps your muscles up:
secrets of the hypotenuse and quadratic equation;
how to drive a car and get a date;
what hormones are, and what they mean to you.

Knowledge pours in: the theme of "Lycidas,"
definitions of *entropy* and *spirochete;*
how deep to bury a dead dog.
Abstractions—*justice, social interest, love*—

weigh you down like rolls of fat,
along with the urologist's phone number,
the lawyer's fee, atrocities of the Khmer Rouge
and CIA, the real reasons your wife married you.

You're mountainous by now—a freak, out of control.
Walled in by books, crushed by printouts,
circuits on overload, not only can't you leave your room—
you couldn't get out of bed if you wanted to.

KATHY EVANS

Psychic Healers

I never liked the anteroom of my analyst's office,
all those Indian relics against beige, an
ashtray from Harrah's in Reno, swag light
on dim, and piles of old *New Yorkers,*
which I flipped through furtively for the captions
under the cartoons, for any kind of humor.
The quiet was palpable, and I could feel the weight
of the San Francisco fog lean against her office door.
Once she fell asleep in a session. I did not
wake her. Compliant, complacent, I allowed her to dream
her own Jungian dreams—dark men in four o'clock shadow;
a red hibiscus opening; anima, animus. I merely
sat there in the leather chair, studied the bones
in her wrists, and yammered rhythmically on and on,
mantra-like, about sex, death, and my pathological
tardiness. The Navajo rug as a backdrop,
her cocked head could have been the perfect
Andrew Wyeth; Helga lines around the eyes.
When she woke, I did not mention that she'd dozed,
nor for how long, because of (you know) the transference-
counter-transference thing. I merely said at the end
of the session: My dead father stands each night
at the foot of my bed. Every day I walk through
a different Bay Area shopping mall in a tennis skirt.
I hate summer. Things die. And just last week
I put my sleeping infant on a cot inside a display tent
at Big Five, and left her there. Am I having a nervous
breakdown? "No," she said, standing dim and fatigued
next to her shelf collection of cactus and succulents,

"You are experiencing what we call a personality
disintegration."
"Oh, good" I said, "I feel so much better, and what
do you advise?" Be good to yourself, she offered,
take a friend to lunch, long walks to the beach,
hot baths, and go to a good Chinese restaurant. So I did.
That hour. I walked back to my car, and drove along
the panhandle of the park, along the boulevard
of churches, down into the Tenderloin, past Macy's
and the flower carts on the corners of Union Square,
down into the financial district. I parked the car
in a tow away zone, phoned Mary on the 16th floor
of the Transamerica Building, and while waiting for her
to descend, watched a stunt man scale the outside
of the pyramid, as if it were one of the high peaks
in the Himalayas. Mary emerged through the double
glass doors wearing a fabric of roses. She looked like a
Queen Anne chair, and I needed to sit. She insisted
instead that we walk through Chinatown. The walk would
do me good, so we strolled up Grant—windows of whole
chickens and cheap silks, back alley smells of wet garbage,
fried won tons and dim sum, tables of trinkets and souvenirs:
Chinese pajamas, carved elephant tusks, flimsy flip-flops,
until we came to the restaurant. "This is it," Mary said.
I half-expected an epiphany. We sank into a red vinyl
booth, unwrapped our chopsticks. I fingered the chrome
napkin holder. "Mary," I said, staring down at the sweet
and sour, "I am experiencing a personality disintegration."
"A what?!" she asked, cupping her tea. "Just shut up,
and open your fortune cookie." So I did. But nothing
was in it, not a single strip, and my purse was gone.
Mary picked up the tab, and when we walked back to the car,
it was gone, too. I looked up. The gray sky was immense.
The man on the outside of the building was a mere speck.

After that day, I quit seeing my analyst.
Summer was summer, and her rates went up.

But two weeks later, a man phoned to say he'd found
my purse. It had been left on a bench in Washington Square.
He was calling to return it. Imagine! to return it!
I drove into the city to meet him, stood on the corner
of Columbus and Broadway with a hand-scribbled sign
that read: The missing purse lady. A man with a pink
face, a cherubic smile, and a bottle in his jacket
pocket shuffled up and handed it over. Of course,
I expected everything to be gone, a sign of further
disintegration. Instead, when I unzipped the oversized
bag, everything was there. Everything—and more:
white finger bowls, spoons, fireworks, rubber snakes,
Chinese slippers, a deck of cards, three watches,
and a jade snuff bottle. A shoplifter, a purse-snatcher,
crafty as hell, moving right up through Chinatown
with my purse! How propitious! I kissed the wino,
handed him two of the watches, the snakes, the snuff
bottle, a full deck, and slapped down in his palm
the only twenty I had in the bag. He smiled and slurred
abundantly. We embraced on Broadway. "Thank you,
I said, "thank you." The late afternoon sun bounced
off the windows of the distant office buildings.
Light fell over the pyramid. Someone switched on
the neon, and I felt fine, just fine.

NATHALIE F. ANDERSON

Desire

We drove out to the city of the dead
where he showed me how the fire blazed through.
You can trace its path over the flagstones,
up the black brick steps still braced by iron
rails and pickets, out onto the cold slab

of the foundations. The heavy trees stand
charred clean, burnished. A palm crests the hill,
its fronds crisped to stubs, its fat bulk bronzed
to a pineapple finial, announcing
hospitality. No rule to it—

how it eats one house and spares another,
skipping this tiled roof and that stained window.
A small-boned cat might kindle in a breath,
but here he comes, mewing for his supper,
and here is a widow, come to feed him.

So he said to me, now you've seen it.
Would you still wake the dragon? Around us
the scorched earth cracked its hoard, every rise bright
with basket-of-gold, hyacinth, lapis, pearl.
Ash lit my tongue. God forgive me, I said yes.

JESSE LEE KERCHEVAL

Glass House

My fourth grade teacher
lived in one.
This is not a metaphor,
she took the class
there on a field trip.
Small strangers in gloves,
we stood outside,
looking in.
You could see
in every room
except the bathroom.
Each so neat, so perfect,
beds made, drawers closed,
pillows fanned
across the couch,
it looked like no one lived there.
Then we filed in,
the door a bridge
from our world into hers.
From the inside,
the outside was nothing
but green trees.
A bird skimmed by,
risking everything to take a peek.
Our teacher showed us
how she used pictures of hawks
to keep the birds away,
cutouts held to the glass
by suction cups

tighter than a man holds
his wife in a house
where more than squirrels
can look in.
Inside the house,
no one said a word.
On the way back,
I remember we sang.

BARBARA HAMBY

The Word

In the beginning was the word, fluttering out into syllables
    like a deck of cards on a table in Vegas,
lovely leafy parts collapsing into atoms and cells,
    genus and phylum, nouns, verbs,
elephants, orangutans, O Noah, you and your philological
    filing and filling of arks, gullets, daughters.

In the beginning was the word and it was as big
    as Aretha Franklin after "Chain of Fools,"
long as your mother's memory of all your misdeeds,
    wide as Jerusalem, a fat-lady-in-the-circus word,
a Siberia, a steppe, a savanna, a stretch, a Saturnalia,
    the party at the end of the world.

In the beginning was the word and we knew which way it went:
    left to right in English, right to left
in Hebrew, an orientation so profound that sexual climax
    is coming in all right-moving languages
and going in those advancing left, though in the moment
    we rarely know whether we are coming or going.

In the beginning was the word, and it was small and perfect.
    Like a Hans Holbein miniature, a dormouse,
a gnat, a bee, a blink, a breath in the lungs
    of Jehovah, Brahman, the Buddha, Ra,
because all the big kahunas of the universe surfed
    in on the crest of that first wave,

and Thomas Edison said let there be light
    and the dinosaurs groaned in their graves,

and there was Albuquerque, late-night roadhouses,
    blues, cigarettes, fish-net stockings,
high-density sodium street lights that blot out the stars,
    cars, diners, the neon urban carnival before Lent,

and Marie Curie said let there be more light,
    and there was radium, radiant thermonuclear
incandescent explosions, Herr Einstein's dream,
    Herr Oppenheimer's furnace,
London burning with Hitler's fire, Dresden cremated
    in the answering flame, *Hiroshima mon amour.*

I ask you, what is this world with its polyglot delirium,
    its plain-spoken, tight-assed, stumble-bum euphoria?
Explain time, for I am fretting on the outskirts of Odessa,
    with Chekhov, with Eisenstein, with ten thousand martyrs
of various unremembered causes, and we are cold,
    hungry, tired of playing Hearts.

Where are you, my minister of *informazione,*
    Comrade Surgeon, Mister Wizard, Gino Romantico?
Can you in your lingo ferret out the first word? Inspect
    your dialect for clues, my Marlowe, my Holmes, your patois
for signs, your pagan vernacular, your scatological cant,
    your murmuring river of carnal honey,

for in the beginning there was darkness until you came,
    my pluperfect anagram of erotic delights,
my wild-haired professor of vinissimo and mayhem,
    emperor of Urbino, incubator of rhythm, blue-eyed Apollo
of the late-night bacchanalia, and there was music,
    that heady martini of mathematics and beauty.

For I am empty, I am full, I am certain, I am not,
    for in the beginning there was nothing
and it was blank and indescribable,
    a wave breaking on the north shore of the soul,

but as every canyon aches for its sky, I burned for you
 with a fever, with a frenzy,

I was a woman craving a blaze, a flame,
 a five-alarm fire in my heart, in my bones,
my hair red as a hibiscus, like a burning bush,
 I was Moses screaming at God,
filaments of flame eating my eyes,
 my sex, the hard sweet apple of my mouth.

MARK HALPERIN

Webs (I)

they are the banners of desertion . . .
        —Primo Levy

They pulse as they catch a stirring
        of air, breathing or rippling,
the shaky outlines of lungs. Beaded,
        they glint with dew when outside,
under eaves, soffits. And when they're in

        attics, dry and still, faint light
diffused by them, they're desiccated, frail
        as the powdery fall leaves pressed
among old letters, ties between a time past
        and breezes, relic and gossamer,

in spite of us. They're symmetrical even
        to where they're spun, in the cellar's
damps and depths as well, the useless dark
        from which the children hurry back,
malevolent and fearful tanglings, no longer

        thought of as spiderless but lines
joining us to things alive, the sticky juices,
        the passions we are and dissolve in,
as if the banners of desertion flown all around us,
        all along, finally acknowledged as ours.

ROBERT COLLINS

Making Love at the Budget Host Motel

Like water rising in a cistern
seeking its own level
I wake up sensing trouble
in the dark of 3:00 a.m.
and hear a woman whimpering
beyond the scrim of motel wall.
I listen closely for a moment
before I figure out it's the couple
in the next room making love.
Several times I overhear them
rise from wasted passion
into a sweaty furor as they start
and stop and start again,
their wooden bed frame pummeling
the flimsy wall between us.
He looms over her in darkness,
furious, determined that she'll
make it all the way to him this time.
She lies out of breath beneath him
about to please her husband
with a gift she's never had before to give.
Perhaps the strange surroundings—
being on the road a thousand miles
from home the same way I am—
the freshly laundered sheets and scent
of Camay soap, and a few too many
cocktails over dinner have convinced
them that this time will be different.
I should stop my ears and turn

away from any scene this sacred,
but I hold my breath and root for them,
wanting her to make it for us all.
For a moment far from home,
her desperate cries rising to crescendo
we three are all united,
as she comes as close as anyone
can come without actually coming.
Then without a sound from him
as though it were unmanly to give
utterance to pleasure, it's over for the moment.
We lie back down in silence,
our separate despairs, our terrible aloneness.
Feeling that I've failed her too,
I fall asleep a second time, wondering
what it is that love requires,
what word or touch that we withhold,
which, if we could freely give it,
might bring us all to ecstasy.

KATHERINE SONIAT

Coming into the River Parishes

Under certain flood conditions in the 1800s the Mississippi began to change its course and fill the shallow Atchafalaya, threatening to turn the land between Baton Rouge and New Orleans into a lagoon.

I

Up in north Louisiana,
the place names grew out of change:
Hard Times, Water Proof, New Roads—
and the little lake-stop someone stepped
out upon, and called it Providence.
Then there's False River calling
each sure declaration into question.

To the south, waterways become
amorphous in the marsh, stream beds
soothed into *estuary, bayou* and *slough;*
rivers rhythmic as the Comite, the Amite,
Tchefuncta and Bogafalaya, on down
to the Atchafalaya. That's the one
that almost missed becoming a river;
for years a seasonal trickle
where the Mississippi dropped off
the leftovers of spring.

II

Under thickets of magnolia,
vine-clog of scuppernong and muscadine,
fur-bearers prowled as the principal parties,
paddling streams tinting from brown

to a pale clay-red.
Out of this confluence of color,
where the Red and the Mississippi met,
the Atchafalaya started a new flow south;
this backwash now a river to think about—
its waters swimming with fishy emissaries,
gar and gaspergou under a sky dark with ducks,
bullfrogs broaching their bass song
for something old in a world gone to change.

        III
It's hard to say how
the world does change.
The old timer at the ESSO station
in Krotz Springs says he's seen it all
come and go, swears the Atchafalaya
swam off with his childhood
while he watched the turn of the century
wheel in on French's Showboat with its floating zoo
of elephants, tigers and lions. In those roars
he suspected the earth growing small,
could almost smell the diesel soon to saturate
the wind. Shaking his head
at "that river" as if it were his
small, unknowing child,
he's off in the flood of '27
telling how afterwards the new-fangled
locks and levees all but laid out rivers to dry.

The ESSO sign bangs in the wind.
It's a toss up as to whose world
dries up and whose washes away.
The old man's talking of mornings
when those engineer-men come to set
their tools up on the levee still,
trying to figure how that trickle once
deepened and, with no help from them,
the Atchafalaya rose in the green magnolia shade.

GRAHAM DUNCAN

The Silence We Cannot Imagine

When I hear the rooster's cry
pulled from his throat by the sun,
I hear in his vocal strut
the umbilical resonate,
source deeper than cord
or lung, the egg's harmonics
before beak breaks through
and gapes, the plucked string
that links all audibles
and the quark's
inaudible twang:
all waves above and beneath
ear's range, the strum
under flux, friction,
break, release, and cry,
all groaning, all crowing,
the unhearable flowering
and falling of the stars,
the grinding of galaxies,
our echoes traveling
the indifferent ether,
the tick that we join
in our dissolution,
that we think but cannot hear,
whose silence we cannot imagine.

DEBRA MARQUART

Somewhere in a House Where You Are Not

There is sunlight coming through windows
somewhere in a house where you are not.

An old man and old woman eating breakfast
to the sound of the clock, out of words,

empty of thoughts, but for who died this year
and of what. If you follow the sun to that house

you will find the long lost driveway
that no highway intersects, the loose gravel

crackling under your wheels, the sun breaking
cleanly free of a horizon. You must park.

You must come to an absolute halt
outside the house where you are not,

letting your many necessary miles drop
from your bones like dust. Sit and wait.

Do not fear the mop-faced dog. He pounds
his tail for you. He is uninterested

in your tires. The old woman will soon come,
peeking through the ancient blinds, saying,

who on earth, and seeing your face
will hold out her hands, warm and soft

as good black dirt, and take you inside,
the house filling with your arrival,

the old man smiling his surprised skeleton smile,
the old woman asking, have you come far,

was it a long drive, are you hungry, are you
tired, to which you may answer, yes

and lie down in the bed they have kept
empty in your absence, reserved for the day

you would need this room full of nothing,
but rare morning light, and the stroke

of an old brown hand, inviting you
to rest, to sleep, to feel the earth

revolve slowly around and around
without you.

NEAL BOWERS

A Legacy

In the photo I've never seen,
she holds baby great-grandfather,
braids hanging over her shoulders.
I think she's beautiful,
though my mother,
who tells me what she was told,
says only "full-blooded Cherokee,"
under her breath, as if swearing
at a spot that won't come out,
claims the cousin who owns the picture
won't show it anymore,
may have thrown it away
with a load of old shoes
and closet clutter.

Because white turns the whole spectrum away,
it is the color of absence,
a condition defined by what it's not,
as in "We are not Indians."
Strange to hear my relatives
who have so little wanting even less,
mistaking emptiness for the brimful cup,
the whole Irish-English lot of them,
dirt-poor and Southern-proud
for who they think they are,
only one generation away
from hired-hands and sharecroppers,
only three away from the woman in the picture.
The younger ones hang Confederate flags

above their beds, bolt "Forget, Hell!" plates
to their cars and trucks, forgetting.

To save anything from oblivion,
it must be named
and called into the world.
Old grandmother, I name you now
and call you out of my own need,
a name that sounds like weeping but means
leaves on a still morning,
or the silence after rain.
Buried once for death
and once for who you were,
your second grave deeper,
lower than love and under memory,
you have withstood tons of darkness,
waiting, compressed to brilliance.

I can see, in my mother's face,
the face I've never seen in the old picture,
sharp-boned, stern, but with a softness
in the eyes, a tender patience—
or maybe I imagine this,
the blood so distant and diluted.
For my own portion,
I have the true inheritance,
the disease that proves the lineage,
diabetes, skipping generations,
killing my grandfather at 35,
a dependable randomness
pointing you . . . not you . . . me.
Overtaken by the past
in the middle of my life,
I have finally become mortal,
feeling in my veins the blood
of a fallen race.

Sometimes, when it's late and the body
lies down with itself,
wanting a better truce with death
than this balance on a needlepoint,
she waves from the dark rim
webbed in a sweet fatigue,
and calls me by the name
I answer to in dreams,
and I answer.

REBECCA McCLANAHAN

Passion Week, 1966

In the sanctuary of fundamental *no's*,
so much was not allowed.
What was left pressed hard
to free itself, the way
even a modest breast, laced
into a bustier, surprises

with dollops of flesh.
It was the week of Christ's
suffering and release. A ceiling fan
paddled the heat as voices of boys
in the pew behind me wandered
the lower octaves. One tenor had legs so long

he could stretch his feet to mine,
which slipped out of white pumps
at first touch and stayed
through hymns and prayers
and the miracle of bread
into flesh. The altar portrait

was a savage Jesus—wilderness hair
and shoulders bare and muscled,
the kind of body God the Father
might have kneaded from clay.
Parents nodded in their accustomed pews
while those of us cast in new bodies

leaned into the story of the son's
earthly side, the women

who loved him. His mother, of course.
The sisters of Lazarus. The whore
who anointed his feet with kisses
and tears, dried them with her hair

and rubbed oils that might have been sold,
the disciples said, to feed the poor.
And Christ, dusty and tired
and not long for this world, rebuked
her rebukers, claiming a higher charity
and suffering the woman to do it.

JAMES KIMBRELL

The Trouble Now

It has nothing to do with the clouds of the last sky,
Or the rain of this one, or the storm-glazed
Arrival in between, which made, for a moment,
The world seem sudden, replete with all
The dilapidated walls and window-lit alleys
In the valley across Yong Island, this life disguised
As the next. Nothing to do with the sound
Of the ocean through my window, with the trunk
Unpacked in the corner, with the salt smell
Of this night, or the crickets that trailed me
All the way from Virginia. It hardly seems relevant
Now that the women at the top of the loose
Stone steps speak a language I don't half know.
Even my radio, so adept at transmission, fluent
And oblivious, bleats out the message—again
You are *here,* again you understand so little.

BILL BROWN

Mounding Potatoes

The phone call at 2 a.m.
was my sister saying
that you had died in
the emergency room
but had been shocked
to life so that your pulse
stabilized and you told
the doctor you remembered
the whole event, heart stopping
and the sharp electric trip back.

He said that such a memory wasn't likely.
But you stuck to your story
even during the ambulance ride
to the medical center where
magical balloons sailed
their timely voyage through your blood
to stretch the vessels
which clogged your heart.

Mother, today you smile at my concern,
knowing what death is like.
At eighty-two, you heard
no voices from beyond,
no angelic music fluttering
a heavenly welcome.
Your faith was stuck
in the strength of this world
as the frantic voiced commands

and the laying on of fire
kept you in life's routine.

Two weeks later, I marvel to watch
your strong hands mound
young plants in my garden,
dreaming the while
of new potatoes with parsley,
resurrected
from this simple ground.

MICHAEL CHITWOOD

Singing Hymns to Go to Sleep

"Jesus, lover of my soul," she sang to me,
"let me climb the telephone pole,
                        if the pole begins to shake
let me down for Michael's sake."

Where my name was
                was a blank
and she would fill in the whole
                   family before I drifted off.

She said Old Scratch.
She said "Elk"
            in the back of her throat
when something surprised her.

She said any water was deep enough to drown you.

"Jesus, lover of my soul,"
               you could sing it
as long as you had names.

We took turns sleeping with her.
After we looked under the bed,
               she would tell a story.

There were three children.
They went into the woods
even though their mother said not.
They met an old woman.

The old woman had a crooked stick.
The old woman said "Children, Children."
She had cages behind her house,
big cages.
The cages had birds the size of dogs.
The woman fed the birds in pans like you cook in.
The birds clopped their beaks like horses walking.
The woman said to the littlest one,
"Do you want to ride a bird?"
She gave the bird a dose of something.
Then the bird had feet like a hog.
A hog will eat little children.

She said that was enough.
She said she thought she heard a rat.
She said if a mockingbird hollered at night
somebody's blood would poison.
"Jesus, lover of my soul,"
$\qquad\qquad\qquad$ she sang to me.
I gave the names.
If you forgot somebody,
they would die the next day.

CLAUDIA EMERSON

Preserves

In the dim noon of the root cellar
the stone walls weep cold tears, but my mind's
on supper as I shuffle heavy
jars of beets, peach halves, snaps, tomatoes.
Nothing looks good in this light. The jars
I didn't fill line the bottom shelf,
and a slight shadow there draws me down.
What drew a mouse into the empty
black mouth of an extra jar? Once there,
how long did it pedal against smooth,
invisible walls in full sight of all
it had left behind, of all it could
not reenter? The skeleton reminds
me of a ship in a bottle, sails
furled, its ribs a fragile hull, the skull
a socketed prow bound to take on
nothing as it cuts a static sea.
The preserved essence of this journey
may not be taken now, however
much I crave it. I quickly choose blood-
red beets and suddenly brighter peaches.

Stable

One rusty horseshoe hangs on a nail
above the door, still losing its luck,

and a work-collar swings, an empty
old noose. The silence waits, wild to be
broken by hoof-beat and the heavy
harness slap, will founder but remain;
while outside, above the stable,
eight, nine, now ten buzzards swing low
in lazy loops, a loose black warp
of patience, bearing the blank sky
like a pall of wind on mourning
wings. But the bones of the place are
long picked clean. Only the hayrake's
ribs rise from the rampant grasses.

LISA ERB STEWART

Words for the Body

The body's never light enough, never
clean enough, or still enough. The body
never went to school or followed Jesus.

The body never has enough to do—
just watches the ceiling, the pillowcase.
The body's always knowing it will die

no better than its own laundry. Because
the body thinks nothing—not even what day
it is. Or its name. Or where it lies

waiting to be touched by another body.
The body doesn't care whose body.

ANDREA HOLLANDER BUDY

Permission

When you have stood at the door
longer than two friends ought to,
one of your mates upstairs
tucking children in, the other
out of town; and when you stand
not gazing off into any distance
at all, recognizing that there
isn't any distance that wants
attention, except the three or four
inches between your face and his, that
that is the distance you'd like
permission to disclaim, erase, void,
you stop.

You step back, find something
simple and unnecessary to do
with your hands, hoping you won't
touch his arm or his face, hoping
he won't move any closer,
that he'll discover something
in the way, something that will
sway him somewhere else; or you hope
words will come, right words
that will shape what is necessary
to shape, so you can keep this
the way you want it: the wanting
and the stepping back. Not the finishing,
not that. As though the *right* words,
if you could find and say them, could really

save you, save you from saying what is
not right, like *yes* or *yes* or especially
the *yes* that is not spoken, which—with
or without permission—you seem already
to be saying nonetheless.

WAYNE JOHNS

First Kiss

> *. . . an invisible veil between us all. . . .*
> —Anne Sexton

November nights steal in so suddenly they catch me,
and all the houses in the neighborhood, off guard,

leaving the street blackened as if the power has gone out.
Just as abruptly, windows snap on—yellow squares

that shadows drift across. I keep sitting in the dark,
holding the invitation to Craig Stevens' wedding, remembering

how we crept up to lit windows those summer nights of 1983.
I didn't give a damn about any of the girls we spied on,

just ached to wedge against him under those rectangular screens
of light, feeling the surge when our arms brushed.

If we were ever lucky enough to see Michelle Poss undressing
or Heather Owens stepping into the shower,

Craig would adjust himself, sometimes even slip a hand
inside his sweat pants. Out of the corner of my eye

I watched, pretending to be excited by the small pink buds
on their chests, the triangles of hair between their legs,

thrilled only by this secret between us. Me and Craig,
dressed in black, imagining we'd mastered the art

of invisibility, like on *Mission Impossible*.
We'd drop flat on the lawns when they heard us

and opened their front doors. That happened a few times.
I couldn't stop shaking, like the time we tongue-kissed—

the rush of it—doing what we thought was wrong.
Afterward, we threw rocks at streetlights

while bats dove into those halos, alive with insects.
They don't really see the light. Something draws them to it.

R. T. SMITH

To Write the *New Yorker* Poem

I need white wine and an open
window, a well-stamped passport
and nostalgia for exotic places
which I have visited (though not
on vacation). Ennui is useful
if it leads to a story, and light
is half the battle, all the better
if shadowed by firs and the tracery
of winter hardwoods. Smoke from
a French cigarette as it curls
toward that light and the cold
lying damp on the sill. A theory,
also, is requisite, something modest
about how our questions shape us,
wind across wheat of an unusual
color. A cast of family villains,
the dispassionate appreciation
of dysfunction, scenes in Manhattan
restaurants. No birdsong
will serve my spell, exactly, but
Stevens' stillness after, perhaps,
and the leafless vines, birdnet
growing green on the fig limbs,
arachnid in this season. But now
I begin to lose it, to see fine
webbing across each image, fact
toiling toward some symbol against
my natural grain. I am close to

meaning something.
     Still, I have
my wine and window, an attitude
of receptive languor, the designer
boots and a midden of prudent
sighs, this trail of ink blue under
the moon's china, a red sweater
knitted by candlelight, cooled
by the blue mountains of Spain.

WILL WELLS

Hard Water

The pipes shudder and spew a tainted stream.
Hard water. My mother seems to keep
it like a Sabbath: tub baths one inch deep,
rigid towels, and tea with flakes of scum.

On my infrequent visits, I submit
to her economies. Widowed ten years,
she's tightened habit down till few can bear
its torque, still unwilling to admit

age greases us to loosen and let go.
She repeats an elegy of bills, the costs
depleting her. But the scrapbook insists
on my success: clippings and class photos

pressed under plastic, for history is prone
to fray or crumble. Our conversation
is a dust disturbed, motes of words that turn
a moment in the light, here and then gone.

A radio preacher's voice drawls between us,
praising devotions as a "golden chain."
Ours is forged by the dint of drips, the stain
under faucets spreading its gospel of rust.

Side by side, we stand at the kitchen sink.
She scours each piece of family silverware,
and I, in turn, dry with elaborate care,
at home in the exiles we cannot forsake.

B. H. FAIRCHILD

Body and Soul

Half-numb, guzzling bourbon and Coke from coffee mugs,
our fathers fall in love with their own stories, nuzzling
the facts but mauling the truth, and my friend's father begins
to lay out with the slow ease of a blues ballad a story
about sandlot baseball in Commerce, Oklahoma decades ago.
These were men's teams, grown men, some in their thirties and forties
who worked together in zinc mines or machine shops or on oil rigs,
sweat and khaki and long beers after work, steel guitar music
whanging in their ears, little white rent houses to return to
where their wives complained about money and broken Kenmores
and then said the hell with it and sang *Body and Soul*
in the bathtub and later that evening with the kids asleep
lay in bed stroking their husband's wrist tattoo and smoking
Chesterfields from a fresh pack until everything was O.K.
Well, you get the idea. Life goes on, the next day is Sunday,
another ball game, and the other team shows up one man short.

They say, we're one man short, but can we use this boy,
he's only fifteen years old, and at least he'll make a game.
They take a look at the kid, muscular and kind of knowing
the way he holds his glove, with the shoulders loose,
the thick neck, but then with that boy's face under
a clump of angelic blond hair, and say, oh hell, sure,
let's play ball. So it all begins, the men loosening up,
joking about the fat catcher's sex life, it's so bad
last night he had to hump his wife, that sort of thing,
pairing off into little games of catch that heat up into
throwing matches, the smack of the fungo bat, lazy jogging
into right field, big smiles and arcs of tobacco juice,

and the talk that gives a cool, easy feeling to the air,
talk among men normally silent, normally brittle and a little
angry with the empty promise of their lives. But they chatter
and say rock and fire, babe, easy out, and go right ahead
and pitch to the boy, but nothing fancy, just hard fast balls
right around the belt, and the kid takes the first two
but on the third pops the bat around so quick and sure
that they pause a moment before turning around to watch
the ball still rising and finally dropping far beyond
the abandoned tractor that marks left field. Holy shit.
They're pretty quiet watching him round
but then, what the hell, the kid knows how to hit a ball,
so what, let's play some goddamned baseball here.
And so it goes. The next time up, the boy gets a look
at a very nifty low curve, then a slider, and the next one
is the curve again, and he sends it over the Allis Chalmers,
high and big and sweet. The left fielder just stands there, frozen.
As if this isn't enough, the next time up he bats left-handed.
They can't believe it, and the pitcher, a tall, mean-faced
man from Okarche who just doesn't give a shit anyway
because his wife ran off two years ago leaving him with
three little ones and a rusted-out Dodge with a cracked block,
leans in hard, looking at the fat catcher like he was the sonofabitch
who ran off with his wife, leans in and throws something
out of the dark, green hell of forbidden fastballs, something
that comes in at the knees and then leaps viciously towards
the kid's elbow. He swings exactly the way he did right-handed,
and they all turn like a chorus line toward deep right field
where the ball loses itself in sagebrush and the sad burnt
dust of dustbowl Oklahoma. It is something to see.

But why make a long story long. Runs pile up on both sides,
the boy comes around five times, and five times the pitcher
is cursing both God and His mother as his chew of tobacco sours
into something resembling horse piss, and a ragged and bruised
Spalding baseball disappears into the far horizon. Goodnight,
Irene. They have lost the game and some painful side bets

and they have been suckered. And it means nothing to them
though it should to you when they are told the boy's name is
Mickey Mantle. And that's the story, and those are the facts.
But the facts are not the truth. I think, though, as I scan
the faces of these old men now lost in the innings of their youth,
I think I know what the truth of this story is, and I imagine
it lying there in the weeds behind that Allis Chalmers
just waiting for the obvious question to be asked: why, oh
why in hell didn't they just throw around the kid, walk him,
after he hit the third homer? Anybody would have,
especially nine men with disappointed wives and dirty socks
and diminishing expectations for whom winning at anything
meant everything. Men who knew how to play the game,
who had talent when the other team had nothing except this ringer
who without a pitch to hit was meaningless, and they could go home
with their little two-dollar side bets and stride into the house
singing *If You've Got the Money, Honey, I've Got the Time*
with a bottle of Haig and Haig under their arms and grab
Dixie or May Ella up and dance across the gray linoleum
as if it were V-Day all over again. But they did not.
And they did not because they were men, and this was a boy.
And they did not because sometimes after making love,
after smoking their Chesterfields in the cool silence and
listening to the big bands on the radio that sounded so glamorous,
so distant, they glanced over at their wives and noticed the lines
growing heavier around the eyes and mouth, felt what their wives
felt: that Les Brown and Glenn Miller and all those dancing couples
and in fact all possibility of human gaiety and light-heartedness
were as far away and unreachable as Times Square or the Avalon
ballroom. They did not because of the gray linoleum lying there
in the half-dark, the free calendar from the local mortuary
that said one day was pretty much like another, the work gloves
looped over the doorknob like dead squirrels. And they did not
because they had gone through a depression and a war that had left
them with the idea that being a man in the eyes of their fathers
and everyone else had cost them just too goddamned much to lay it
at the feet of a fifteen-year-old boy. And so they did not walk him,

and lost, but at least had some ragged remnant of themselves
to take back home. But there is one thing more, though it is not
a fact. When I see my friend's father staring hard into the bottomless
well of home plate as Mantle's fifth homer heads toward Arkansas,
I know that this man with the half-orphaned children and
worthless Dodge has also encountered for the first and possibly
only time the vast gap between talent and genius, has seen
as few have in the harsh light of an Oklahoma Sunday, the blond
and blue-eyed bringer of truth, who will not easily be forgiven.

BECKY GOULD GIBSON

Laying Out the Dead

Day's catch-basin deepens, filling.
You've come to help the others
in a room with no air,
the stink of rotting vegetables.
The woman is cold, fish-fleshed.
You wring out a vinegar cloth,
travel the body: scaly neck,
nipples gone to hair, slack belly,
thighs, labia rubbery, raw-gilled.
The dead have nothing to decide.
Had she been through the change,
put away boiling rags,
her pearly roe used up?
Rhythm in your palms,
you rub on verbena oil
to give a light sheen.

Death never leaves the dead,
merely sinks into layers,
silt packing the creek-bed.
You hold a lamp
while someone coils the hair.
He'll find his wife changed,
laid out on the crocheted spread,
cleaner, lonelier
than she's ever been.

Yourself still, shivering,
you step to the porch,

moon-rinsed pines, owl's
quickening cry. Someday hands
will wash you, tend your death.
And you'll take that current
as the woman has done,
running, running
the cold river like a trout.

JUDITH TATE O'BRIEN

Not Counting the Men

The number of those who ate was about five
thousand, not counting the women and children.
          —Matthew, 14:21

On the sixth day God created Eve and later
fashioned Adam to be her fit helper. Suppose

God called Sarai to set out for Canaan, and Abram
tagged along, shamed, unable to beget. Suppose

the covenant was marked by menstruation,
and semen made men untouchable, unclean. Suppose

Miriam led the Jews out of Egypt, and when Moses
complained "Does God speak only to women!" the Lord

struck him with leprosy. Suppose boy babies counted
for nothing except sperm. Later, the story might

go, Jesus called twelve women, and no one wondered
about families they left behind. Suppose Jesus

led the prayer "Our Mother who art in heaven,"
and according to Matthew, Jesus multiplied

loaves and fish and fed a crowd of 5000—
not counting the men. Suppose Aquinas

admitted in the *Summa* that, well, yes, men had
souls—temporal ones. And what if, Her Holiness

Ellen Marie IV in Rome penned Latin encyclicals
explaining why God doesn't want men ordained.

As an exercise, just suppose . . .

RANDOLPH THOMAS

Finishing the Puzzle

Probably by now, my neighbor, who bought
the jigsaw puzzle at my yard sale,
has started working it.
               She has no doubt
studied the picture of the carefully-
tended English garden on the box.
She has emptied out the pieces in the box,
arranged them into piles by shapes and colors.
Looking at the picture, she cannot help
but think how hard someone has worked.
Someone has trimmed the hedges, watered
the roses, given the garden an aura
of stately perfection.
               At some late hour,
perhaps tomorrow night, working alone
while the neighborhood sleeps, she will discover
that the final piece is missing. By then
I will have gathered what the bank has left me,
loaded up a borrowed station wagon, kissed
this neighborhood goodbye—enough of this.

But even if the woman tracked me down
I could not tell her more than that the piece
was never there, that even on the night
when I first slit the paper, opening
the box, the picture had been incomplete.
I would remind the woman that the hedges
in her garden are well-trimmed, the roses
watered, clipped until the petals look like

thin strips of plastic, redder than any roses
I have pulled my back muscles tending.
                                        It
is doubtful she will ever track me down
or even try, and I hope that when she
learns the truth, at three a.m., bent over
a card table, beneath a pale lamp, she
can push the puzzle aside; that nothing
in her life, recalled by that missing piece,
will drive her to her knees, to search the floor
by flashlight; that she can laugh easily
and call the puzzle finished as it is.

LYN LIFSHIN

Did You Know I Love You

the first words
my mother says
waking from
demerol. The
iv tangles
like outlines
into a knot
that stops the
flow. "Honey,
are you ok?
Are you
hungry? Did you
sleep?" Her
voice blurs,
thick. "Are you
ok, honey?" My
mother, who can't
get to the bath
room alone jokes
one day when I
reach for her,
"are we dancing?"
and must put
her hands around
my neck to be
pulled off
the toilet,
worries I couldn't
sleep   wants

to she says
if I could
carry her to
my bed, rub
my back

KATHRYN KIRKPATRICK

Crossing the Border

1.

Behind the machine gun,
through the bullet-proof visor,
I might have met his eye
from the rented car with Dublin plates,
from beside my English husband,
from the line of Ulster Protestants
I'd come from, almost here,
this very ground.

Weaving through traffic in Derry
we'd somehow got between
two armored cars
with English soldiers hunched over guns.
And then those automatics
swiveled onto us.

I'd heard a Belfast woman
on call-in radio
say a soldier worried his trigger
whenever she hurried past. *Walk fast*
she'd been instructed. *Don't look at them.*
But something keeps me staring
into the rifle barrel.

2.

We walk the streets of Derry
in the dusk, the fortressed inner city,
the shops on the town square

all barricaded by steel doors
against bomb blasts
and at the city center, a monument
to soldiers in World Wars,
an odd omission of the fighting here.

In front of Guild Hall
we stand, awkward beside
the cannon-riddled wall,
reading the town history, official,
and not so clear, or so allusive
as the words we read spray-painted
on the panopticon:
FAWK BIG BROTHER—WHO'S WATCHING WHO?

3.
From Limavady and Colraine,
from Castlebar and Ballymoney,
on and on they came,
the Protestant bands
in cobalt blue berets with orange plumes,
Men of Ulster, Pride of Ulster,
with their military faces,
their strange, unseeing stare,
a few accordions, some snares
but mostly marching men with flutes
and the drummer beating wildly.

They teach their young
the loud, fierce beat, each band
with boys beside the striding
grown men and one so young
bewildered by the sound—
what did he hear as he stumbled
to keep time, almost trampled
in the turning?

In front of us, a young man
cheered, gave thumbs up
to the men he knew
and danced from street to curb
punching the sky with his fist.
His half-empty lager rolled
into the street and tightlipped
a woman lifted it from among
the marching feet
onto the windowsill.

    4.
Up the last ridge
to our Appalachian home
with the sky ripe and furred
as a peach. *Gloaming.* The word's
in my ears like some tribal memory.
Here is where the Scotch-Irish came
three hundred years ago
from County Antrim and Tyrone,
rackrented, then indentured,
stowed in the bowels of boats.
They came as we come now, weary but grateful
for this mountain-shouldered sky.

But the first night home
when I dream myself in red curls,
I pull them off to the black lengths
of my great-grandmother's hair,
a Cherokee, from among these hills
where I now live, driven
to Oklahoma in tears.

I am that hybrid,
American, firing the shot
that pelts me. I am
that other,

a woman, who always makes
her own country,
furrow and brick,
mortar and till.

STARKEY FLYTHE JR.

Paying the Anesthesiologist

Which doctor put you to sleep?
the accountant asks when I phone,
and I think of lectures,
conversations, sermons,
of how easy it is to glaze
somebody else's eyes
when our own vision
is so clear. I remember the nurse
putting her finger up
to my lips and vanishing, the self
waking up a thousand years—the money,
too—later, body black
and blue in odd places
that had nothing to do—
not that any part of me had anything
to do—they breathed, swallowed, beat
in my chest, I had only to lie
there, free even of my dreams—odd places
that had nothing to do with the operation. I
was grateful to be alive, surprised
the way a wild animal finding himself
in a city might be, staring at the red
sign that flashed, Walk. Or, like being
impatient with an airplane forgetting
how long trains or worse, wagons
took. What is memory but the counter
of time? Where I went I could take nothing,
not even Newton's laws. I swam armless,
a fragment of Greece, plaster taking on

water, the bottom dizzyingly close, blindly
bumping into walls dead to the sound
of pain, splicing. Praise hands
that shook over my face, spleen that broke
my fall. Sing mainly, quietly sleep.

GWEN EBERT

American Insomnia

There will be no dogs in heaven barking at night.
There will be no night, for which I am grateful,
and no sleep, which makes this moment almost heavenly.
It's a way of looking at things, say, L.A.—or the empty car
being towed in the other lane and how lonely it is without the usual
head at the wheel. On airport escalators we seem so American,
looking at each other and looking for evidence of what we are
or should be. No one tells. No one claims their solo version
of humanity. No one invites the others in to rest on the beaten sofa.
We will not tease each other as if we were alike in embarrassing ways.
It's not a joking matter, the weight, the divorce, how we sit at the feet
of Madison Avenue and ask the television over and over if this
is being alive, or is that, and will you play it for us again
in another set and wardrobe? Can we believe the crowd
of voices in the living room, bringing their drama and their cool?
Saturday night the saxophone crawls like a snake,
smooth as cappuccino in Manhattan.
We can almost believe we are having a good time.
We can almost believe Talk Radio as a kind of neighborhood.
Pieces of family are left like derelict farm machinery in the stodgy states.
Our deli food comes ready made in take out trays for one.
And one and one, everywhere, America in its choice, does not know
what to wear, when to laugh, how to love, how long.
Awkward as a digital clock—a money machine, angry as traffic
we are strung together by the high voltage buzz of our need.
It's on 24 hours a day, tireless as a glacier.
By strip malls and video stores it has eaten the landscape as a snack.
Now we cannot sleep. The old wilderness is gone
and a new one howls at night,

worse without predators and silence,
without mystery and soul—
more immense, more lonely, more inexhaustible.

5

The 2000s

In 2002, *Southern Poetry Review* made a move as significant as Guy Owen's relocation of the journal from Florida to North Carolina in 1964. After Robert Parham accepted the position of editor, *SPR* came to Savannah, Georgia, from Charlotte, North Carolina, and as discussed in the introduction, the shift led to key changes in format and editorial style. Although Parham left Savannah in 2004 to serve as dean of arts and sciences at Augusta State University, not far away, the journal remains housed at Armstrong Atlantic State University, where it receives assistance but maintains independent status. It operates with its smallest staff ever, but one as committed as any before it: Robert Parham in Augusta, and in Savannah, two professors at AASU, James Smith, associate editor, and Tony Morris, managing editor, as well as invaluable student assistants. We modified the journal's format but kept Owen's eclectic ideal. *SPR* reaches individual subscribers, bookstores, and libraries (more than ever before) in all regions of the country, as well as abroad, and finds its poets in those diverse places, too. We routinely challenge our editorial inclinations, discussed below, in a decade that has made it particularly urgent to be clear about guiding principles.

The official end of the second millennium passed without major incident. Americans had inured themselves to news of suicide bombers and terrorism abroad in the 1990s, but on September 11, 2001, the attack on U.S. soil brought home an unalterable perception. Security was an illusion. During the shock and grief, the anger and fear that followed, the country turned in surprising numbers to poetry for consolation, and literary journals, including *Southern Poetry Review*, received innumerable poems attempting to give voice to trauma. "Security" is a watchword for the decade.

This ancient theme stands out starkly during this decade because of 9/11. Several poems in this section directly evoke that specific day: Katherine E. Young's "HAZMAT," Peter Makuck's "Matins," and Cathy Smith Bowers's deftly misleading "For Okra." However, many poems published after the event, and not focused on it at all, feel charged by it and its aftershocks, even Philip Dacey's humorous paean to the New York Public Library's Main Reading Room ("New York Postcard Sonnets, #6"), which describes a haven for people of the word.

Also during this decade, Enron and other financial scandals shook everyone's faith in corporate pension plans—and corporations, in general; HIV was now global; the threat of global warming intensified; Katrina hit New Orleans. The list goes on, but 9/11 epitomized the American sense of safety lost forever.

In the late 1980s and early 1990s, tempests over "New Formalism" rattled teapots on both sides of the debate. The turn to form after 9/11 was more instinctual, however, less programmatic than before. During this time at *SPR,* many writers submitted poems in traditional forms or poems distinctly formal, counterpoise to the chopped-up prose of much contemporary poetry. For most of them, form is not a post-9/11 revelation. But the sheer number of powerful sonnets (Amy Fleury's "At Twenty-Eight"), poems in rhyming quatrains (Jay Rogoff's "Mysteries"), rhyming couplets (Stephen Gibson's *"Profile of a Young Woman"*), and poems with exacting visual patterns (Suzanne Cleary's "Anyways," David Citino's "Shovel," Fleda Brown's "Trillium," David Kirby's "Someone Naked and Adorable") all attest to the contemporary viability of distinct form. Too, this section is full of poems in free verse that measure their lines with acuity. This close attention to our language always has mattered, but maybe it seems to matter more intensely now.

Southern Poetry Review continues to seek the carefully crafted poem, language not in the service of an idea so much as an idea in service of the language. We want to notice the language and the form before the idea, or best, at the same time—craft inseparable from insight. We also prefer poems with some narrative framework. Who speaks and out of what circumstances? (The current fad of glib non sequitur makes us yawn.) Often, this scaffolding is minimal. We rarely publish pure narratives. By contrast, we rarely embrace the lyric mode that tends toward glossolalia.

Although *Southern Poetry Review* never has been clubby, continuity with poets across the decades reminds us of what we value: not a message or agenda, not regional affiliation, not fame. *SPR* prizes the artful poem, the poem attentive to itself and the world. When the journal has found such writers, it has encouraged their return. A survey of this book will reveal many of them. During the 2000s, we have renewed contact with and published the latest work of many poets from previous decades of *SPR*, some of whom appear in this section. We also trust that poets published by *Southern Poetry Review* for the first time during the 2000s will send us their poems in the decades to come.

The section opens with "Anyways," a poem of serious humor by Suzanne Cleary, which defies the trauma theme by asserting a stubborn resistance (in its form, as well) to loss and the fear of loss. Several poems evoke the tenacity, and tenuousness, of the nonhuman natural world and remind us of our interdependence and the perils of forgetting it—for example, Kathleen Flenniken's "Richland Dock, 1956," about a poisoned river. Too, in its exacting syntax, Robert West's "Toll" re-creates a familiar, yet always startling scene: a creature in our headlights. Its "safe passage" in the final line cheers us. The section and the book conclude with "Door," by longtime contributor Chana Bloch, whose poem recounts a symbolic experience that asserts no creed or belief, but which attempts to appraise uncertainty, then leaves us, like the speaker, on its threshold.

SUZANNE CLEARY

Anyways

for David

Anyone born anywhere near
    my hometown says it this way,
        with an *s* on the end:
            "The lake is cold but I swim in it anyways,"
            "Kielbasa gives me heartburn but I eat it anyways,"
        "(She/he) treats me bad, but I love (her/him) anyways."
Even after we have left that place
    and long settled elsewhere, this
        is how we say it, plural.
            I never once, not once, thought twice about it
        until my husband, a man from far away,
    leaned toward me, one day during our courtship,
his gray-green eyes, which always sparkle,
    doubly sparkling over our candle-lit meal.
        "Anyway," he said. And when he saw
            that I didn't understand, he repeated the word:
        "Anyway. *Way*, not *ways*."
    Corner of napkin to corner of lip, he waited.
I kept him waiting. I knew he was right,
    but I kept him waiting anyways,
        in league, still, with me and mine:
            Slovaks homesick for the old country their whole lives
        who dug gardens anyways,
    and deep, hard-water wells.
I looked into his eyes, their smoky constellations,
    and then I told him. It is *anyways*, plural,
        because the word must be large enough

to hold all of our reasons. *Anyways* is our way
of saying there is more than one reason,
    and there is that which is beyond reason,
        that which cannot be said.
            A man dies and his widow keeps his shirts.
        They are big but she wears them anyways.
    The shoemaker loses his life savings in the Great Depression
but gets out of bed, every day, anyways.
    We are shy, my people, not given to storytelling.
        We end our stories too soon, trailing off "Anyways. . . ."
            The carpenter sighs, "I didn't need that finger anyways."
        The beauty school student sighs, "It'll grow back anyways."
    Our faith is weak, but we go to church anyways.
The priest at St. Cyril's says God loves us. We hear what isn't said.
    This is what he must know about me, this man, my love.
        My people live in the third rainiest city in the country,
            but we pack our picnic baskets as the sky darkens.
        We fall in love knowing it may not last, but we fall.
    This is how we know *home:*
someone who will look into our eyes
    and say what could ruin everything, but say it,
        regardless.

PHILIP MEMMER

Walk

At first there's nothing strange about the sight
of children riding ten-speeds, weaving eights

across the four-lane road, their loops so slow
they have to drag a foot to keep from falling.

But this is not some dare for lulls in traffic—
here come their parents down the center line,

and not at all like suicides or drunks
but speaking casually, their gaze directed

up the road a bit, towards the river.
When was the last time semis shook the windows?

Not recalling, we join the dazed parade
that gathers in the brilliance of the street.

How wide our road's become, and how unknown,
as if this weren't a suburb of New York

but some exotic ruin we are walking—
each streak of oil, each shred of weathered trash

radiates a sacramental calm.
It's heaven, someone laughs—where danger was,

sunshine and stillness, actual wonder.
How quick we are to join this quiet world;

then what we mistook for the hush of a breeze
becomes the swift-clear sound of water

and we see it at last, the river
above its banks and making way

through yards, porches, cars—it's coming
as fast as we can run to what we love.

LOU LIPSITZ

Being, 1

> *Being has not been given its due.*
> —*Jean-Paul Sartre*

let's not
say
too much.

let's
keep
the lines
short.

Being is
quieter
than
poetry

and
needs only

a small
space

like a
spider

legs folded

done
with webs.

PHILIP DACEY

New York Postcard Sonnets

6.

The Public Library's Main Reading Room,
great nave of a cathedral for the bookish.
Listen closely and you'll hear brains hum.
A turning page embellishes the hush.

From the heaven of a ceiling, chandeliers.
Rows of heavy tables invite a feast
of words. Liturgical, the scrape of chairs.
Most heads down; some up, giving the eyes a rest.

Like subway riders: close and distant at once.
Brass lamps spread hominess in Bly's "favorite
room in the world." (From Robert, rare good sense.)
Changing times: each laptop has its outlet.

Risen to glory, the high school study hall!
Cellphone users here get their own circle in Hell.

WILLIAM JOLLIFF

Mose Whipple Says Good-Bye

Now they've taken to naming the streets
after what's been cut or drained. Here's
Pear Orchard Way and Bear Swamp Road,
and every brand of tree from Yellow Poplar

back to Alder. It's a way of remembering,
I guess. Better than none. Beats hell
out of what that last developer did—
every kid or wife he ever had: Amy Court,

Nancy Lane, Roberta Park, and, Lord God,
Della Street. I don't know that it matters.
Seems funny that the only things I'll know
if I come back are the names of what was.

And I don't know who "Florida" was, if anybody,
but I like the sound of her better all the time.
God knows what they'll call this old farm,
but it's theirs now, take it and be damned.

KURT LELAND

Ode

Leaves of three,
let it be.
    —Folk Proverb

Spiteful congregation of inhuman hands! Your stirs,
your frantic genuflections with each wind's passing,
revert to a wrinkled green vellum's soothing
eyeful, whose chance-brushed illuminated scriptures,

written on innocent skin in invisible ink,
will emerge in a week: the purgatorial
itch of ire divine love loves to bestow on all
who trespass against it. Your trinity makes me think,

spreading the month-long frissons of its anointing oils,
that God is that spiritual discomfort whose
blistering center is everywhere, the balm of whose
circumference nowhere. Each fall, when leaf smoke roils

the burnt offerings of unwantedness skyward
and your bread-white flowers have become a waxy
inedible berry-flesh, forewarned about the
grudge that the fenced-in yards' fire-brand-bearing guard-

ian your foliage is holds against us—
an auto-da-fé one can truly glimpse hell through—
I shiver at what the rashness of burning you
would inflict on the soul: an orogenesis

raising its cordilleras, cutaneous crusts
and domed lava-pools, its bursting volcanics,
intolerable epidermal plate tectonics
above weeping rivers of serum, the pink rusts

of Calamine's bentonite magma. No wonder
my best friend's three-year-old daughter, shown just once your
tree-twined red blaze in the backyard's Eden, refers
now to maples and sweetgums as poison. Saviour

in childhood from the hated summer-camp swim lessons,
recruiter of mothers to a lay priestesshood
of scrapings, gauze wraps, and lotions—how we stood
your mostly pointless perpetual temptations

to touch ourselves in all the wrong ways I don't know.
The weight of water as it drops from the shower-
head onto that swelled spot on my shin's a pleasure
as sexual as any deity's sin. So,

much as I loathe your effects, at times I can't see
why you never became some ancient faith's holly,
hedging the sacred with untouchability:
in the sun-burning bush, my God's poison ivy.

CARRIE SHIPERS

Last Time,

I left too much. This time I'm taking
beer bottles, wire hangers, a vase
I mean to repair. I'm folding wallpaper
into lopsided swans, dismantling
light fixtures, peeling paint
from kitchen shelves. I'm sacking
chickpeas and plastic forks,
emptying the dustpan into a blue
glazed bowl. I'm labeling my boxes:
used batteries, fallen leaves,
iris bulbs from the yard next door.
I don't know how to live without
one turquoise earring (not mine),
the ceiling crack that helps me sleep.
I'm running out of room to pack
my nightmares and paring knives,
my knowing glance and everything
I've borrowed: salt shaker, almanac,
little black dress. There's no telling
what I'll need once I'm not here.

GREG RAPPLEYE

Were We Speaking, Had You Asked

I'd bring you cauliflower
and the leaf tips of artichokes.
Or tiny radishes and
wild fennel, the violet ribs
of chard, shorn of all flesh;
sliced ginger root, the woody hearts
of parsnips—acidic, astringent.
You might try the leeks:
one end spring green, the other—
forged in mud—
resplendent, bone white.
You might cut through the pulp
of these purple beets,
splay them across wilted
spinach, swirl them
with turnips, pungent mustard
greens, weedy amaranth
or rapini, slightly past its prime,
sauté them all with olive oil
and chopped garlic.
Are they bitter?
That is something best known
at the root of the tongue, where
muscle and blood run thick,
where the nerve ends *fire,*
fire, fire at whatever starts to gag,
snapping shut the voice box
and binding the heart to silence.

ANDREW GRACE

For Tityrus

who had to, as we do now, watch the neighbors leave,
        us from our porch facing Route 45, pollen drifting

like smithereens from some erupted star over the truck
        of a family whose few hundred acres were taken

not grandly by droves of Octavian's godless soldiers
        fresh from civil war, but by simple hard luck, rootworm

and corn borer, too few loans to afford an acrid cascade
        of insecticide dropped from those planes whose tracers

make the mock-girding which fails each night to prop up the sky.
        Tityrus, who purchased in Rome from Octavian himself

the right to continue to graze his flock in the dropped-apple reek of fall
        between the stunted row of tamarisks and the rock outcrop

that marked his land—if he were here I could ask what advice
        to give as they come up the drive to return the twenty yards

of electric fence borrowed to keep raccoons from their pumpkins,
        what to say to this family whose three fields we will soon try to buy

at the lowest negotiable price, so that it won't be our furniture
        someday sticking out the back of a flatbed. Tityrus,

who offered his neighbor one last night in Arcadia, clover
        for his sheep, chestnuts and cheese for his journey, did more

than we are willing to. It would take more than generosity
        or condolence to stop this father's belief he's been cheated

by those humid nights spent awake urging on the mass of bats
        constellating above their corn, feeding on that which fled

from our well-sprayed land onto theirs, wrecking the yield.
        If Tityrus were standing here with us, watching their exhaust rise,

I would ask him if I should take it as a sign that our farm
        is the last one in the county with its original name, *Shadeland*,

as night falls and my mind latches on only to that
        which is giving itself over to bare and continuous forces—

the unbeautiful pears fallen at tree's roots, evening wind's
        far-off baying, the chipped and gap-bricked mouth of a well

that with each freeze and thaw feeds on itself, increments of stone
        humming beyond earshot into nothing, which is quick, and final.

DAVID HERNANDEZ

Let's Drink Now

This is where the wrecked convene,
and these the stools they plop
their stories on, the pool table
where they rack their worries
and fool themselves: *I make this,*
the test will come back negative.
Ask the peroxide blond
chalking her cue what's eating her
and she'll look up, expose
the scar zippered shut on her neck
where the surgeon removed
her lymph nodes. She sinks
four, five stripes, takes a long
drag from her cigarette, the smoke
blotting out her face. See that man
hunkered by the jukebox?
He drinks until he's a ship
trapped inside a bottle,
sailing towards the sun's cork.
Ask and he'll tell you
it was one dark thing after another:
tunnel, cavern, tunnel, cavern.
Let's drink now. Something
to ignite our embers, heat
for our bones. Round after round
until the floor seesaws,
until the bartender shoves us
into the night and the stars zigzag
over our heads like fireflies
with no idea where to take their light.

ROBERT BENSE

At Kellogg's Landing

I start with the car packed. Urgencies
boxed. There's lightning to the south.
This morning the sacred cows were sent
to slaughter. I no longer advise
on securities. Commodities
have been severed from the malice
of weather. Horses from hands, fat
daughters. The vigil of books behind me.
Works and days. Age's broken pediments.

The alluvial landscape I drive through
accumulates particulars. Children
abandoned. MTV in the school lounge.
Greyhounds shot. Scrutiny peering
from hills sliced by the river I look for.
Behind the wheel I sort out my ruin.
Somewhere, whole wards fearing contagion.
Easy malaise of the bourgeoisie. Promise
of rain seems just. Storms follow water.

The towboat with barge for eight
cars answers the flash of my lights.
I'm the only car but character
follows. Wind whipping up the willows
on the river bank. I cross over to
Missouri. Judgment at my heels.
The passing horn of a tow high sorrowful
out in the current. It's already a dirty river
but I'm running from my life.

ENID SHOMER

"Gowned Waiting"

is the name of the room where we sit, clutching
rouge-pink robes with flimsy ties. One flips

through fashion mags. Her cubicle door ajar,
another rehearses a script, while two friends,

scheduled together, compare injustices
at work. I'm writing this in my journal, trying

for calm against the terror at hand, this visit
a truce with disease I negotiate twice

a year. A woman enters speaking broken
English, weeping. We understand—tears

are the native idiom here in "Gowned Waiting."
Minutes ago, she was swept aboard

the diagnosis express, where everything blurs
like a landscape rushing past, though at the moment

her train creeps so slowly that seconds
freeze, refusing to pass, trapping her

in the instant of discovery, the words
that struck like fangs—*malignant, invasive . . .*

bad. The brochure they gave her—support
groups and hotlines, survivors beribboned in pink—

lists on her lap like a shipwrecked paper boat.
She wants to run the day backwards,

as I did last year. To walk back
out through the clinic door to the subway stop,

to my block, to pause in reverse for the breakfast I grabbed
on the run until I'm standing wreathed with steam

in the morning shower, completely clean.

MARC J. SHEEHAN

A Note on Rejection

When I first fell in love with my ex-wife
I'd take the Amtrak train to Chicago
and must have passed the same backyards that Tunis
Ponsen spent his whole life painting, though it's hard
to stay in love with something for that long.
The broken-fenced back alleys of tenements'
only beauty is the beauty of someone
who's said, *to hell with it, this is who I am.*
And that's not who I was back in '78,
ten years after Tunis Ponsen died
largely ignored after early success,
maybe because his subjects were too modest.
Now his paintings have come out of basements,
and a gallery show reminds me how
the slate-gray waves of Lake Michigan made
the best melancholy background for walking
to Union Station for those Sunday trips home.

In his last self-portrait Ponsen painted
himself without any background at all.
He could be a brown-suited salesman, an
insurance exec or actuarial.
His painting of a cigarette left burning
beside an airmail delivery letter
on a windowsill overlooking rain
makes even the least attentive Sunday
art lover here for hors d'oeuvres stop and look.
Is love contained in that letter, or loss?
Ponsen crafted his palette carefully to

capture the balance of these two people
below his window walking away from
each other in that gray rain. Maybe fame
ain't so great; you don't know how many years
of it you'll have—whereas love and loss are
for forever, or at least your part of it.

HARRIET BROWN

On the First Day of Middle School, My Daughter Walks into a Cloud

A ways from where
I stand, not waving,

she hefts her backpack,
lifts her violin, and turns uphill.

Her deep brown ponytail
bounces with every step,

a flag from childhood
hoisted by the woman

she's becoming. The cloud
swallows her up, backpack

and ponytail and violin—
or maybe it's me

who's swallowed up
and she is walking

through a slant of sunlight,
breathing in rosemary

and forget-me-nots,
running the last few steps

to where she's going.
Maybe I'm the one

in the cloud, feeling my way,
telling myself,

Shh, everything's all right.

KATHERINE E. YOUNG

HAZMAT

After the hazardous materials crew
has cleaned the rooms, I move among familiar
things, touching here and there a vase, a lamp,
straightening the absurdly clean cloth
in front of the baby's place. We are obsessed
with decay, with bodily fluids, inconvenient
remnants of our animal selves. I think
of rabbis in latex gloves scraping the blood
from Jerusalem streets, of the Muslim custom
of burial within twenty-four hours.
Surely the bone hunters and reliquary
makers, the city fathers warring over
John the Baptist's knucklebone had it right:
flesh is Essential. Flesh is Divine.

I subscribe to the religion of airplanes,
silver-winged vessels that transport a person
to realms unfamiliar, where alien temples
ennoble the hair, the nails, the body
and blood of obscure local saints. These are
my relics: a rug rescued from scissors, a cat
plucked from an engine, a book that—once—
would have won its possessor a bullet
in the skull. Some say Death's an angel—this, too,
I have seen—flash of steel wings, whirlwind
of atomized flesh, dust carpeting rug,
cat, book, interior spaces and private
reliquaries, particles of shared disbelief.

CATHY SMITH BOWERS

For Okra

I'd never seen so green a green
before, so lean
those tender pods
I stopped and bought

when I knew for certain you were
not on that plane.
Trish, what would my
selfish life have

been? But no—come get some okra
now. I've dredged and
fried it. Just the
way you like it.

ALLAN PETERSON

Plenty to Go

There is plenty to go around   After all
there are almost two of all of us
split down the middle so we can share blood
and give away kidneys
Even the brain is halved ready to serve

We are built for plenty from the stars down
That's why we're uneasy with mirrors
and dotted swiss and their heavenly excess
pasted or drawn like a scratchboard on the inner skull
a galaxy   discrete streaks of meteors
then all that tangle below

Under their glass domes the clocks
are tightened just enough
to be true to the dozen numbers
they are always touching then leaving
They cannot decide   are constantly in love again
with the next one equally long
with equally slim feet

If we lie down and share these bodies
with the sunny edge of the woods in Meridian
the plentiful grass will cover us so we cannot see
and we will be part of the watery purples
making timely landscapes for someone
long before they get there
The gnats and other grass angels above us
say there is enough for everyone

but you must be finally satisfied
with that one asymmetrical death
and keep it keep it completely to yourself

TEMPLE CONE

Calf-Bearer

I dreamed myself a calf-bearer last night,
one of those giant, rope-veined statues
excavated from the Acropolis,
a brown calf cloaklike across my back.
It was the long day of sacrifices,
the air filled with fearful bleating, the slick stench
of burned guts, and black flies storming above
the grease flames for a taste. This calf, though,
was calm, its fur still sour with morning milk,
the pale, swishing tongue not raspy but soft
as wet cloth on my cheek. Marble steps climbed
to the altar in hundreds, infinite
but nearing end. I gripped above the hoofs,
waiting for tendons to tense, flinch, buck, kick,
but no struggle came. Amid the ringing knives,
I felt only soft ribs sucking in air,
a dank hay scent blowing against my neck
I had fifty more calves to bear up that day.
I remember smiling. I must have been
smiling, distant, archaic, like the marble
statues themselves, whose faces are always
the same, shining, from the terrible knowledge
that sometimes seems like joy, that it is never
their own holocaust to which they go.

GEORGETTE PERRY

Names of Small Fish

Twelve years old, at night I'd wake to
leaps and splash-backs in the square glass tank.
Sometimes I covered it,
afraid they'd leap too high.
They were minnows from a nearby stream,
yellow-brown, with sleek black stripes.

I took them at last
back to their stream and freed them,
when my life was changing,
my mother gone down to dust and whispers.
Or was it earlier, when she was with me
and I still prayed like a child
while she sat by my bed?
Before and after blur across the years.
What prayer is left goes dark:

>Is there no end to your many?
>How can you outrace so many dyings?

Near the park, where stream cuts under street
I stop to watch schools of tiny fish
trembling between shadow and sun.
In the library I search for my striped minnows
as if a name may bring them back.
Too many names! Too many bright flickers
all over the South in "clear fast creeks."
Creation's exuberance, biologists' laughter,
penning poem-names for quick shapes:
stargazing minnow, tongue-tied minnow,

warpaint shiner and cherryfin shiner,
riffle minnow and speckled madtom.
Starhead topminnows rise to kiss the sky.
Flurries of small striped fish dart out of sight.

ROBERT CORDING

In the Garden

I'm mowing the lawn and tidying up
my flowerbeds, thinking of people
just like myself and that guy in Kansas,
a city inspector who went around measuring
the length of his neighbors' grass—

a little odd, extreme even, but all-in-all,
the neighborhood concluded, a decent guy
involved in his church community.
That was before the news of his arrest,
before people learned a serial killer

had lived among them overlooked
for years. At first, they were shocked—
who wouldn't be?—their dreams invaded
by footsteps and a voice so calm and brutal
it woke them to their darkened rooms.

Christ! Is everyone's face a mask?
Even the beloved teacher can turn out
to be a molester, and too often it's that
quiet kid next door who shows up at school
with assault rifles and automatic handguns.

But then the detectives revealed the clues
that, one by one, had added up and lit
the circuitous path straight to the killer's door.
Newspapers discussed the triumphs
of state-of-the-art technology in forensic science,

and thoughts of a killer probing for
his chance on dark streets yielded to the logic
of the day and the sun turning the season
everyone's way again, the streets shining
with ornamental trees and plantings.

MICHELLE DETORIE

Doll House

The tragedy
of the world
in miniature:
teacups, knives,
a sink, a sofa, a bed,
a tiny rectangular
newspaper—inscrutable
marks—a clock,
a fireplace, a crib.

JOAN MITCHELL

Drought

Season of the exoskeleton, spider days
when the black widow flashes her hourglass.

Land of red ant, black stink bug, rustle
of lizard and snake, where the bark beetle carves

intricate galleries into dying pines.

Life dries from the outside in
to tough root and armored stem.

Buds parch before they can bloom.

We, too, turn inward, slow
as the day's heat climbs.

A snake coils at the spigot.

Beyond, the earth chimes light, lacks
past lives for lives to feed on.

The wind wears trees to bone.

Once I thought there were clouds, but it was fire
lively across the valley.

Still, the nights are owl-eyed and cool. Moths
drum against the window. Last winter's snow

drifts green along the arroyo—rabbit brush
and snakeweed, Apache plume and sage.

There are thick-skinned gourds.

And primrose, low to the ground,
miraculous as manna.

PETER MAKUCK

Matins

for David McCourt

A curve of beach, a moon,
    Hunter leaning overhead,
        Surf all boom and seethe.
    I move closer to the lights
Of two barges and a tug at anchor

A hundred yards off the bar—
    A demonic factory
        Pumping back sand
    That's been taken by storms.
I'm walking with the hard news:

Your wife and daughter on the first plane,
    A friend on the second,
        Those fiery undying towers.
    Diesels drone on the barges,
Increasing store with loss

And loss with store—an old line
    Against an edge under siege.
        Dark figures move on the decks.
    I turn away, listen to the surf's
White noise, salt on my lips,

Walk until I'm sleepy again,
    Stars fading in the east, a call
        For prayers, chanting voices
    Lighter than this foam
Blown along hard wet sand.

JAY ROGOFF

Mysteries

Trompe l'oeil triumphant! The architectural
details, the loud Greek key frieze like a maze,
the cool egg-and-dart molding—sleights of space
that make my fingers ache to caress the wall

from yards away, behind the rusting chain.
And yet the frescoed humans register
flat—not all human: brandishing a mirror
a putto waggling wings that look strapped on

clenches crossed legs as if he needs to potty
while the maidservant studying his glass,
performing sacred rituals of dress,
prepares to bind the gold hair of her lady.

Putto and maid look comfortably immured:
nothing they do demands a third dimension;
it's mystifying how little illusion
the painter mustered in a town this cultured,

this sophisticated. Even the matron—
sposa—even the lady has been partly
rendered to provoke shudders: see that clumsy
wrist, how her bent little finger looks broken

and her yellow gown cascades irrespective
of her lower anatomical dimensions.
Yet in the teeth of such incompetence,
in this remarkably uncontemplative

ritual of the morning, she has paused,
half her hair held high upon her head
awaiting the supple fingers of her maid,
to stare at us. It's the first time she has gazed

out from the wall, and on fresh mystery
outside her glass she's fixed her long-dead eyes.
The world's the mirror where we return her gaze,
stunned by the painter's sudden mastery:

her upper arms' ingratiating flesh,
the gauzy nothing of her dress's bodice
which can't conceal a candid breast, unless
it's damage from the baptism of ash

that kept us strangers eighteen centuries.
Above her head, the key frieze yields to crumbling
plaster; below, a line where the earth's trembling
fractured her clavicle. Her curious

expression, calm in its calamity,
with full-fleshed lips like stone, dead as her heart,
cracks no codes, whispers no nothings about art,
wearing the long fault of mortality.

EDISON JENNINGS

The Sympathy of Dust

Her Hoover Vortex Master hums,
the house a diary of dross,
Pop-Tart crumbs, playground grit,
wicked grains of glass
the broom did not pick up
when her boyfriend broke
a long-neck Miller beer,
fragments of a narrative
she tracks from room to room,
cobwebs, dead bees, used-up lipstick,
pollen shed by Easter lilies
one week past their prime,
and later when she cannot sleep,
the nightscape fills with cosmic dust
she heard Carl Sagan talk about
on the old *Tonight Show,*
comet ash and star chaff
settling on her sleeping son
and on the now remembered face
of the whiskey-crippled father
she tried not to love,
how it falls, the dust of genesis,
until she falls asleep at last.

KATHLEEN FLENNIKEN

Richland Dock, 1956

Someone launched a boat into the current,

caught and delivered fish to the lab
and someone tested for beta and P-32.
Someone with flasks and test tubes tested
and re-tested to double check the rising values.

And someone drove to the public dock
with a clipboard and tallied species and weight.
Chatting with his neighbors, *Which fish
are you keeping? How many do you eat?*

And someone with a slide rule in a pool of light
figured and refigured the radionuclide
dose. Too high. Experimented frying up
hot whitefish. No. No. Then someone decided

all the numbers were wrong. Someone
from our town. Is that why we
were never told? While someone fishing—
that little boy; the teacher on Cedar Street—

caught his limit and never knew.

GARY FINCKE

The Sum Total

"Beware the sum total, a thing that bites,"
Miss Hartung said, sounding like a pastor.
"We all are numbers," she said, "just listen,"
Reading us Bible words, speaking for God.

The sum total had perfect attendance;
It growled and bared its teeth when thick columns
Of figures covered the dusted blackboard,
And Miss Hartung called us up and offered
Thirty seconds to work out an answer
Like one thousand, two hundred eighty-four,
The sum total of eight numbers, then nine,
Then ten, carrying 1s and 2s and 3s
While everybody waited for his turn,
From Ronald Ambrose to Anthony Zeck,
Who would clutch the chalk and stare, scribbling
A guess so awful Miss Hartung would press
A finger to her lips to warn us mute.

By April, there were negative numbers
In Miss Hartung's tests. "Look," she repeated,
"These columns are like your lives, all of you,
Don't kid yourselves, because the sum total
Can be zero, or worse, somewhere below."

Now, the ordinary could be counted.
We said minus five for burping, minus
Fifty for throwing rocks through the windows
Of a house left behind, unsold, by death,

Behavior's daily total serious
With fractions and integers to the right
Of the decimal point, not including
The negatives I said nothing about,
The private additions for lust and lies,
Jealousy, laziness, and lack of faith.

So far below zero, so self-absorbed,
I thought my secrecy was singular,
Saying my sums without moving my lips
Like Frank Wertz, who whispered the numbers one
Through six before he opened his lunch box
Or workbook, the sum total twenty-one
As if that sequence finished the small hex
On the routine, unlocking the next thing
While I imagined speaking those digits
Past possibility's enormous page
To the sum total of eternity
That lies at the sudden end of numbers.

RON RASH

Hearth

Two days and a night snow fell,
cold closing on Spillcorn Cove
tight as a bear trap, and held
kin close to their fires until

the eighth day when sun began
to raise their world out of white,
and on the far ridge a smudge
of smoke above the tree line,

proof the old man had weathered
another hard winter though
a nephew went to make sure,
and found the porch, back room gone,

by the hearth one man, what he
decades back raised to surround
granite slab, creek-rock chimney
mainly smoke and hearth-ash now,

crowbarred oak plank by oak plank,
fed to the fire, a cabin
unbuilding itself back to
the stone core where it began.

STEPHEN GIBSON

Profile of a Young Woman

—Piero di Cosimo

The head is in profile. The breasts are targets.
Actually, the nipples. She smiles, and regrets

nothing in this moment. Around her neck is a serpent.
That necklace costs more than anyone has spent

on her—and men have spent everything: seed,
fortune, reputation. She is stingy to their greed,

and they rejoice. She lavishes upon them her pittance
of nothing—they hoard zero. They await the chance

to add nothing to naught. The breeze in the forest,
the sea in the conch—that is lust. She is the test.

Success, they know, means death—the *little death*
of orgasm (in French, *le petit mort*). Her breath

revives the corpse. In her is art, literature. As Freud notes,
also their perversion: violence, war. Piero gloats.

JEANNE MARIE BEAUMONT

Getting to Know You

What is your favorite flower, favorite bird?
I really want you to tell me. If you had twins
what would you name them? Or two goldfish?
How about two cats from the same litter?
Mittens or gloves?
What letter did you most love learning to write
so when you scripted it over and over in your copybook
you tingled with graphic pleasure?
Pick a crayon. What's the best time of day?
When you play *Monopoly,*
which little token represents you on the board?
Have a seat. This could take a while.
Cup or mug? Placemats or tablecloth?
Would you rather live in a world where no one cared?
When you were six, what was your favorite song?
It's sad to forget. Uh huh.
What suit of cards do you prefer? Which fairy tale?
Seashore or mountains? You must choose your horse
on the merry-go-round or you can't ride—a lesson
of long ago. What were the most comfortable shoes
you ever owned? (Here I could tell a strange story.
Let's just say I have evidence each of us
has a foot-double; somewhere there's someone
who could fill your shoes exactly.)
What do you want for dinner?—speak or starve.
My head hurts too.
As it happens, you've stumbled
into my humble democracy.
Here's your cup of coffee, your violet-blue crayon,

your miniature iron, your hummingbird . . .
now, friend (if I may call you friend),
better get to work.

JIM DANIELS

Thorn

Mr. Nobody alone in the corner house
planted picker bushes to keep kids
from cutting across his lawn.

We dove over them at night, muffling
our scratched laughter with grass stains,
thinking we were somebody.

We twirled around his sharp corner
as he smoldered, fat cigar ash dropping
to the tiny square porch.

We were little firecrackers, *pop, pop,*
down the street. Was he a bomb or a dud?
The picker bushes grew taller,

but so did we. *Ouch, ouch,* we laughed.
Years before we understood
his ordinary fuse.

LINDA PASTAN

Thought Upon Waking

What if this ordinary morning
I am waking to (sun tangled
in curtains . . . a confusion
of birds at the window . . .
the scented grace of coffee)
is merely a memory
of some other morning years ago?
What if I turn my head

and you are not beside me,
haven't been for years,
and there is only the whiteout
of your vacant pillow?
This is either fact or prophecy—
my one life no more than a spool
of memories unwinding
into the unpersuaded air.

ELLEN WEHLE

Pine Tree, Mountain

Corkscrewed by wind, shaken
        to flinders. In photographs

she juts from the ledge of rock
        like a scuttled ship, gaunt

hag, burnt spindle. Choosing
        a shot, who would document

such ruin? She says: My love
        is the green foundry. Father

of granite. Cloud-shouldered.
        Dark or light, I know only

the sough of his breathing.

BILL BROWN

Deep-running

She knows that summer
creeps at evening tide:
sloughs receive their herons,
sassafras and willow
frame open water, cypress
stand knee deep in duckweed,
and raccoons seine shallows
for crayfish.

In her heart a cricket sings,
but in her head the hum
of neon wakes her. Light,
always outside her room,
frames the crack beneath
the door, monitors foot traffic,
mop and broom.

She turns on her side
and whispers, *deep-running,*
her father's word for the river
beyond the levee; and then
behooved, the measure
of her mother's code.

She presses her lips tight
to say *pipsissewa,* Cherokee
herb that stays green all winter,
and *persimmon,* smell of sweet
musk on the forest edge in fall.

She mouths these words
when sleep hides until
she drifts like mist on pools
where screech owls conjure ghosts,
and her father stands on a berm,
a night heron, lifting his arms
like wings.

DEBRA A. DANIEL

Hymn of Invitation

This spring they are in style again,
those piqué blouses with buttons in back,
the ones that bare the arms to day-lit nights,
nip the waist, then slit and flit to a coy hemline,
flirting with the earliest hint of hip.

I wore mine first on a Sunday evening,
vespers in a whisper-painted church,
sunset and colored glass in ripe reflection
on the boy next to me in the cushioned pew.
Slanted rays blushed him, stained his hands.

When the lights dimmed for the sermon,
he pulled a pen from his pocket, leaned forward,
drew on the length and meat of his thumb,
a hula girl; and as his knuckles bent and swiveled,
she danced a crimson sway.

His gaze angled at me, brown eyes
so humid, I wanted to lift my hair, let air cool
the nape of my neck. He straightened, crossed
his arms so that his hands were hidden. We sat
not quite touching, the service edging to invitation.

And then his index finger slow and sure as sin
found and grazed my sleeveless skin,
tracing a line down and up, down and up;
while the girl he had drawn lay folded
and curled tight against his palm.

LEE ROSSI

Philip Sleeping

I depict his back because my husband's face
with its abstract, New England
simplicity of shadow and line

would distract from the torso's
weathered creams and blues,
its muscled marble. Notice,

I've confined him to the leftmost
third of the canvas, while the rest,
a seascape of pillows and sheets

tossed by a passing squall, declares
that someone has just left, maybe I,
but more likely, one of the women or men

whose need for his beauty is more physical
than mine. Whoever it is, I want you to feel
him—solid, opaque, unmoved.

You will say, perhaps, the work seems cool
and think to yourself, cruel, a bit callous,
a child worrying some belovéd pet.

But who will remember what he was
when all the world desired him?
How vivid the bedclothes, how restless,

breaking in waves against his dreaming form.

ARTHUR SMITH

Golden Gate

All the known jumpers off the Golden Gate
Chose to face the known Bay
And not the towering cold Pacific.
There are witnesses. You can understand

Wanting to, trembling out there
On braided cables, wind-whipped
Hundreds of feet in the air. From that height,
Water has the density of rock. It's surprising

A handful have lived. Any one of them
Would tell you jumping is an act
You have time to reconsider.
In a heartbeat, they knew.

DAVID CITINO

Shovel

Nonno fits a hand to the top of my head.
    I'm a prince. "*Come sta?*" I know the answer
        to the question, when it comes from him:
            "*Bene, bene,* I'm good, Pop." W. 105th, Cleveland.
        He and Nonna live up, Uncle Dominic
    and his family, down. In the garden out
back, the grape arbor a tunnel to Calabria,

purple stars shiver in evening foundry breeze.
    Railroad ties span 52 years on the B & O. Stink
        of creosote marks the plot. A peasant Adam, he
            makes words with magic stones. "Hey, boy: *Fico,*
        fig," he intones, tossing a pebble with care as if
    this scrawny scrabble is the Tree of Life. "*Aglio,*"
pebble, "garlic," aromas my friends mock me for,

and "*pomidoro,* tomato." Nonna will put up
    in jars the *marinara* laced with basil leaves,
        oregano, thyme to last Ohio's winter, a life.
            He shows me the beauty of the shovel. I climb
        the blade top, first one step, then the next.
    Ground breaks beneath my feet, oldest scents.
I balance on the ache and hope of work.

PAUL GUEST

Libretto for Insomnia

The world is so much an orphan of matter,
and love, if I could tell you only this:

that the stars are the night's poor stewards,
that the lost looking up see dark only

and find in all that radiant cold
a shadow of guidance, a poor song—

then I would have said enough
to quiet the thrumming of the sad earth

like an engine, for a time, for an hour,
for enough time to dream of some other life

and begin to see it as my own.
And in that life a distant music

full of bells and light as ash
would cover me like a blanket, as you do

some nights when the world
is all winter's pang, a ringing ache

in every socket. In my mouth
are the right words, I know,

but I can hardly bear them tonight;
I am hungry, and tired—

for nights now sleep has barely come.
Waiting, one hates it

more than it is right. Rising up
to air from almost drowning,

the nearly dead, heavy with a last life,
hate the taunting light

until it breaks upon them
and their life returns once more.

From the edge of my bed,
I can see a few things:

the time lighting the wall a dim red,
the curtains gossiping

in the heat rising from the floor,
and beyond them a light

so faint it must be the dawn.
Or the moon, stirring

the water that bathes the world.
Love, perhaps it is fire.

I will tell you when I know.
I will tell you everything.

AMY FLEURY

At Twenty-Eight

It seems I get by on more luck than sense,
not the kind brought on by knuckle to wood,
breath on dice, or pennies found in the mud.
I shimmy and slip by on pure fool chance.
At turns, charmed and cursed, a girl knows romance
as coffee, red wine, and books; solitude
she counts as daylight virtue and muted
evenings, the inventory of absence.
But this is no sorry spinster story,
just the way days string together a life.
Sometimes I eat soup right out of the pan.
Sometimes I don't care if I will marry.
I dance in my kitchen on Friday nights,
singing like only a lucky girl can.

DAVID KIRBY

Someone Naked and Adorable

When I see the sign that says "Nude Beach,"
           I scuttle right over, though when I get there,
all I see is three guys who look like me,
           two in baggy K-Mart-type bathing suits
and one in a "banana hammock" of the type favored
        by speed racers and the lesser European nobility,

and as they wait for the naked people to appear,
           all three scowl at the sand, the water,
the very heavens themselves, the clouds
           as raw as the marble from which Bernini
carved the *Apollo and Daphne* whose bodies rang like bells
        when the restorers touched them,

like the bells of Santa Croce that summer
           that woke me and Barbara every morning
in Florence, which we called, not "Florence,"
           but "Guangdong Province," because
Hong Kong was in the news a lot in those days,
        and Hong Kong is near Guangdong Province,

and the bells would go *guang! dong!* as though
           a drunken priest were swinging from the bellrope.
Now surely that is "the music of the spheres"
           (Sir Thomas Browne) as opposed to
"the still, sad music of humanity" (Wordsworth),
        which is just some guy playing a violin in the corner.

Or four guys: a string quartet, and not a good one, either,

            one that meant well but hadn't practiced
very much, or maybe one that hadn't even
              meant well, that just wanted to get paid,
maybe meet a scullery maid or two,
        perhaps a nymphomaniacal marchioness. . . .

What the hell do people want, anyway?
              Why does Barbara adore the cameo I gave her
that depicts Leda and the swan, an episode
            in interspecies relationships that just gives me
the creeps? There must be something there
       about being, not dominated, but overcome—

about allowing oneself to be mastered
           by a force greater than oneself
or just another person who has taken on
           temporary godlike powers,
for life has a sting in its tail, like a chimera,
       and you can no more draw that sting yourself

than you can tickle yourself,
           whereas another person can do both.
Why, in the "cabinet of secrets"
         of the Archeological Museum in Naples,
I saw a bell in the shape of a gladiator at war
       not with another warrior but with his own *Schwanz*!

It had rolled up on its back,
          if a penis can be said to have a back,
and was clawing and snapping at its master
         with the nails and teeth of a lion!
And in turn he, the gladiator, was slashing back
       with a broadsword in one hand and some kind

of lion slapper or *Schwanz* slapper in the other!
         Slap, slap, slice, slap! That would sting,
wouldn't it? And it's a bell, remember,

     so the whole was meant to be struck
and struck hard, be it by angry bachelor
   or vengeful wife! Dong! And given the choice

of which part of the bell to strike,
      who wouldn't strike the pecker-penis,
the ravening lion of unrequited desire?
     As if to say, *you're* the one who's causing
all the problems, *you're* the one body part
   who's making trouble for all the others!

No, no, we want something else altogether,
     for, as wise old Mr. Emerson says in
A Room With a View, Love is not the body
     but is of the body, the one we are waiting for
there on the beach, rooted in the sand like shore birds,
   our every atom tingling with desire.

JAMES SCRUTON

The Names of Birds

Flicker. Grackle. Coot.
Ruby-throated this, red-headed that,
downy or belted or crested.
They swirl, excited syllables,

feathering our speech like oaths
out of Shakespeare: thou nuthatch,
bufflehead, worm-eating warbler.
Thou pied-billed grebe.

Skylark and nightingale flown,
give me something local
and down to earth, flycatcher
or thrasher, a working-man's bird,

and, for the two of us, names
as light on the tongue as on the wing,
names to make a love-nest of
my little widgeon, my chickadee.

FLEDA BROWN

Trillium

named for its trinity of leaves, of petals

The universe prefers
    odd numbers. It leans,
        obsessed with
what's next. It likes syllogisms,
    the arguments of
        sonnets: if A
equals B, then C.
    The ground-level
        common denominator,
the blood-red whorl
    at the base, is not
        an answer but
a turning. Does that leave you
    dizzy? What can I
        say that would
reassure either of us? Even
    our prayers have to
        catch hold
as if we grabbed a spoke of
    a merry-go-round and tried
        to convince
the universe of what we want
    stopped, reversed.
        What it gives us
instead: this bad-smelling
    beautiful bloom.
        "Let go, let go,"
is what it says, and who wants
    to hear that?

ROBERT WEST

At a Loss

for Robert Creeley (1926–2005)

There's no telling
what needs
saying.

Toll

A late-
and low-crossing
pair of eyes

flashed in our headlights
like small change—

enough to buy
something
otherwise shadow

safe passage.

VERONICA PATTERSON

Retriever

The sleek wet head of a dog bobbing—no—
pulsing forward, wake not smooth
as a muskrat's V, the dog
not quite dolphin except in glee,
draws me to water. The world has
so many seams—this dog slips me
back to ideas about rapture
and longing—no—not *ideas,* but *skin*
and sun and buoyancy, smell of water,
algae, trace of oil, fish. Where are the borders
I count on between this day and another
dog, swimming for a stick thrown into the lake,
simplified head just above the surface,
ears plastered back as if gills.

Four children laughing
call the collie "Ralph, Ralph Beauregard,
Ralph Beauregard Bugleboy," but he will not stop
leaping into Cayuga Lake. Stick into water,
dog swimming, stick again, dog again, stick, dog,
throw and fetch in exuberant cahoots, just as
one day plots with another, *now-me*
with *then-me* keen for a stick
she—no—I want to throw, and a dog
to carry it back like news, to a shore
where he begs to go again. The heft of it,
stick or childhood, the retrieval. The sheen
and effort—no—all sheen. Wet stick
that has never broken—soaked, arcing
into the air, who's going, who's
going into the buoyant day?

CHANA BLOCH

Door

I knocked on a door and it opened.
That's the moment
he keeps coming back to.

—The door was half-open?
No, the door was shut,
I didn't think anyone was there.
—Then why did you knock?
There was a stranger who knew me at once,
who said, "Yes, come in."
—But why did you knock?
I was tired by then,
it was Friday, late afternoon,
I had given up trying.

He can't tell me
what made him pause
at that juncture of self and door—

I know that place. More than once
I've walked past it, looking
at my watch. Or I stopped

but did not knock.

Contributors

Betty Adcock. She has published six books of poetry. Her most recent is *Slantwise* (Louisiana State University Press, 2008). Adcock teaches in the low-residency Warren Wilson MFA Program for Writers.

Paul Allen. His most recent collection is *Against Healing* (Salmon Poetry Ltd., 2008). Allen is a professor of English at the College of Charleston in South Carolina.

A. R. Ammons (1926–2001). He wrote more than twenty volumes of poetry, including the posthumously published *Bosh & Flapdoodle* (Norton, 2005). He was a professor emeritus at Cornell University, where he taught from 1964 until his retirement in 1998.

Nathalie F. Anderson. Her most recent book of poetry is *Crawlers* (Ashland Poetry Press, 2006). She is a professor of English and the director of the Creative Writing Program at Swarthmore College.

Philip Appleman. He has published seven volumes of poetry. His most recent is *New and Selected Poems, 1956–1996* (University of Arkansas Press, 1996). Appleman is a distinguished professor of English at Indiana University.

James Applewhite. He has published eight books of poetry. His most recent is *A Diary of Altered Light* (Louisiana State University Press, 2006). He is a professor of English at Duke University.

David Axelrod. He has published three books of poetry. His most recent is *The Cartographer's Melancholy* (Eastern Washington University Press, 2005). His poems have appeared in *Alaska Quarterly Review, Boulevard, Kenyon Review, Quarterly West,* and *Willow Springs*. He is the associate editor of *basalt*.

Coleman Barks. He has published six books of poetry and is the translator of *Essential Rumi* (HarperCollins, 1995). Barks is a professor emeritus at the University of Georgia.

Gerald W. Barrax. He has published five books of poetry. His most recent is *From a Person Sitting in Darkness: New and Selected Poems* (Louisiana State University Press, 1998). Barrax is a professor emeritus of English and the poet-in-residence at North Carolina State University.

Dorothy Barresi. She has published three books of poetry. Her most recent is *Rouge Pulp* (University of Pittsburgh Press, 2002). Barresi is a professor of English and creative writing at California State University, Northridge.

Jeanne Marie Beaumont. Her two books of poetry are *Curious Conduct* (BOA Editions, 2004) and *Placebo Effects* (Norton, 1997). She teaches at the Unterberg Poetry Center of the Ninety-second Street Y and in the Stonecoast MFA program.

Robert Bense. His most recent book of poetry is *Readings in Ordinary Time* (Backwaters Press, 2007).

Simeon Berry. His poems have appeared in *AGNI, American Letters & Commentary, Chelsea, Crazyhorse, Green Mountains Review, Hayden's Ferry Review, Iowa Review, Southeast Review,* and *Verse*. Berry is a poetry and fiction reader for *Ploughshares*.

Wendell Berry. He has published sixteen volumes of poetry. His most recent are *Window Poems* (Shoemaker & Hoard, 2007) and *Given* (Shoemaker & Hoard, 2006).

Chana Bloch. She has published three books of poetry. Her most recent is *Mrs. Dumpty* (University of Wisconsin Press, 1998). Bloch is a professor emerita of English at Mills College, where she was the director of the Creative Writing Program.

Joe Bolton (1961–1990). He wrote three books of poetry: *Breckenridge County Suite* (Cummington Press, 1989); *Days of Summer Gone* (Galileo Press,

1990), published posthumously; and *The Last Nostalgia* (University of Arkansas Press, 1999), published posthumously, edited by Donald Justice.

Jody Bolz. Her collection, *A Lesson in Narrative Time,* was published by Gihon Books in 2005. Her poems have appeared in *American Scholar, Indiana Review, Ploughshares,* and *Women's Review of Books.* She is an editor at *Poet Lore.*

Cathy Smith Bowers. She has published three books of poetry. Her most recent is *A Book of Minutes* (Iris Press, 2004). Her poems have appeared in *Atlantic Monthly, Georgia Review, Kenyon Review, Poetry,* and *Southern Review.*

Neal Bowers. His most recent book of poetry is *Out of the South* (Louisiana State University Press, 2002). Bowers is a distinguished professor of English at Iowa State University.

P. C. Bowman. His chapbook, *The Museum of Childhood,* was published by the University of South Carolina Press in 2008. His poems have appeared in *Kansas Quarterly, Northwest Review, Poetry,* and *Virginia Quarterly.*

Catharine Savage Brosman. She has published six books of poetry. Her most recent is *Range of Light* (Louisiana State University Press, 2007). Brosman is a professor emerita of French at Tulane University.

Bill Brown. His recent chapbooks include *Tatters* (March Street Press, 2007) and *Yesterday's Hay* (Pudding House, 2006). His poems have appeared in *Borderlands, Louisville Review, North American Review, Prairie Schooner, South Carolina Review,* and *Tar River Poetry.*

Fleda Brown. She has published six books of poetry. Her most recent is *Reunion* (University of Wisconsin Press, 2007). She is retired from the University of Delaware but teaches in the Rainier Writing Workshop low-residency MFA program at Pacific Lutheran University in Washington.

Harriet Brown. Her chapbook is *The Promised Land* (Parallel Press, 2004). Her poems have appeared in *North American Review, Poetry,* and *Prairie Schooner.*

Andrea Hollander Budy. Her most recent book of poetry is *Woman in the Painting* (Autumn House Press, 2006). Her poems have appeared in *Crazyhorse, FIELD, Five Points, Georgia Review, Kenyon Review, Poetry,* and *Shenandoah.* Since 1991, Budy has taught as the writer-in-residence at Lyon College.

E. G. Burrows. He has published four books of poetry and five chapbooks. His most recent chapbook is *Sailing as Before* (Devil's Millhopper Press, 2001).

Kathryn Stripling Byer. She has published five books of poetry. Her most recent is *Coming to Rest* (Louisiana State University Press, 2006). Byer has served as the North Carolina poet laureate since 2005.

Turner Cassity. His most recent book of poetry is *Devils and Islands* (Ohio University Press, 2007). Cassity retired as a librarian from Emory University Library, where he worked from 1962 until 1991.

Fred Chappell. He has published twelve books of poetry. His most recent is *Backsass: Poems* (Louisiana State University Press, 2004).

Michael Chitwood. He has published six books of poetry. His most recent are *Spill* (Tupelo Press, 2007) and *From Whence* (Louisiana State University Press, 2007).

David Citino (1947–2005). His final book of poetry was *A History of Hands* (Ohio State University Press, 2006). Citino was the poet laureate at the Ohio State University, where he taught for over thirty years.

Suzanne Cleary. Her two books of poetry are *Trick Pear* (Carnegie Mellon University Press, 2007) and *Keeping Time* (Carnegie Mellon University Press, 2002). Cleary teaches at SUNY Rockland in Suffern, New York.

Judith Ortiz Cofer. Her most recent collection of poetry is *A Love Story Beginning in Spanish* (University of Georgia Press, 2005). She is a professor of English and creative writing at the University of Georgia.

Billy Collins. His most recent book of poetry is *Ballistics* (Random House, 2008).

Robert Collins. His most recent book of poetry is *Occasions of Sin* (Mercy Seat Press, 2005). Collins teaches literature and creative writing at the University of Alabama, Birmingham, where he directs the creative writing program and edits *Birmingham Poetry Review.*

Temple Cone. His two chapbooks are *A Father's Story* (Pudding House Press, 2007) and *Considerations of Earth and Sky* (Parallel Press, 2005). His poems have appeared in *Green Mountains Review, Louisville Review, Midwest Quarterly, Nimrod, Poem, Poet Lore,* and *Southern Humanities Review.*

Robert Cording. He has published five books of poetry. His most recent is *Common Life* (CavanKerry Press, 2006). Cording is Barrett Professor of Creative Writing at College of the Holy Cross.

Philip Dacey. He has published eight books of poetry. His most recent is *The Mystery of Max Schmitt: Poems on the Life and Work of Thomas Eakins* (Turning Point, 2004).

Ruth Daigon. Her most recent book of poetry is *Handfuls of Time* (Small Poetry Press, 2002).

Debra A. Daniel. Her poems have appeared in *Emrys Journal, Gargoyle, Inkwell,* and *Tar River Poetry.*

Jim Daniels. His most recent books of poetry are *In Line for the Exterminator* (Wayne State University Press, 2007) and *Revolt of the Crash-Test Dummies* (Eastern Washington University Press, 2007).

Phebe Davidson. Her most recent books of poetry are *Twelve Leagues In* (Spire Press, 2006) and *The Drowned Man* (Finishing Line Press, 2006). A distinguished professor emerita at the University of South Carolina in Aiken, Davidson is also the founding editor of Palanquin Press.

Michelle Detorie. Her poems have appeared in *Blackbird, Chelsea, Caketrain, Confrontation, DIAGRAM, Notre Dame Review, Poetry East, Potomac Review,* and *Verse Daily.*

James Dickey (1923–1997). He published over twenty volumes of poetry. He served as the poet-in-residence and a professor of English at the University of South Carolina in Columbia from 1969 until his death.

Annie Dillard. Best known for nonfiction (*Pilgrim at Tinker Creek* won the Pulitzer Prize for general nonfiction in 1975), Dillard has published two collections of poetry: *Tickets for a Prayer Wheel* (University of Missouri Press, 1974) and *Mornings Like This* (HarperCollins, 1995).

Mark Doty. He has published seven books of poetry. His most recent is *Fire to Fire: New and Selected Poems* (HarperCollins, 2008).

W. S. Doxey. He has published a chapbook. Doxey is the editor and publisher of *Notes on Contemporary Literature.*

Graham Duncan. His most recent collection of poetry is *Every Infant's Blood: New and Selected Poems* (Bright Hill Press, 2002).

Stephen Dunn. He has published fourteen books of poetry. His most recent is *Everything Else in the World* (Norton, 2006). He won the Pulitzer Prize in 2001 for *Different Hours* (Norton, 2000).

Gwen Ebert. Her two books of poetry are *The Little Bat Trainer* (Four Way Books, 2002) and *The Twig Songs* (Parallel Press, 2001).

Claudia Emerson. She has published four books of poetry. Her most recent is *Figure Studies* (Louisiana State University Press, 2008). She won the Pulitzer Prize in 2006 for *Late Wife* (Louisiana State University Press, 2005). Emerson is a professor of English and the Arrington Distinguished Chair in Poetry at Mary Washington College in Fredericksburg, Virginia.

Kathy Evans. She has published three books of poetry. Her poems have appeared in *Alaska Review, Atlantic Review, California Quarterly,* and *Oberon.*

B. H. Fairchild. He has published four books of poetry. His most recent is *Local Knowledge* (Norton, 2005). Fairchild is a professor of American literature at Texas Christian University in Fort Worth.

Jean Farley (1928–1974). Her book of poetry *Figure and Field* was published in 1970 by the University of North Carolina Press. Her poems appeared in *Kenyon Review, New Yorker, Poetry, Sewanee Review,* and *Southern Review.*

Gary Fincke. His most recent book of poetry is *The Fire Landscape* (University of Arkansas Press, 2008). Fincke serves as the director of the Writers Institute and professor of English and creative writing at Susquehanna University in Selinsgrove, Pennsylvania.

Kathleen Flenniken. Her first book of poetry is *Famous* (University of Nebraska Press, 2006).

Amy Fleury. Her first book of poetry is *Beautiful Trouble* (Southern Illinois University Press, 2004). Fleury is an associate professor of English at Washburn University.

Starkey Flythe Jr. His two books of poetry are *They Say Dancing* (Ninety-Six Press, 2003) and *Paying the Anesthesiologist* (Ninety-Six Press, 1998).

George Garrett (1929–2008). He published eight books of poetry, including *Days of Our Lives Lie in Fragments: New and Old Poems, 1957–1997* (Louisiana State University Press, 1998).

Becky Gould Gibson. Her most recent books of poetry are *Aphrodite's Daughter* (Texas Review Press, 2007) and *Need-Fire* (Bright Hill Press, 2007). She teaches at Guilford College.

Stephen Gibson. His two books of poetry are *Masaccio's Expulsion* (MARGIE/IntuiT House, 2007) and *Rorschach Art* (Red Hen Press, 2001). His poems have appeared in *Epoch, Georgia Review, Notre Dame Review,* and *Southern Review.*

Albert Goldbarth. His most recent book of poetry is *The Kitchen Sink: New and Selected Poems, 1972–2007* (Graywolf Press, 2007).

Andrew Grace. His first book is *A Belonging Field* (Salt Publishing, 2003). His poems have appeared in *Boston Review, Crab Orchard Review, Denver Quarterly, Iowa Review, Poetry, Poetry Daily,* and *TriQuarterly.*

Paul Guest. His two books of poetry are *Notes for My Body Double* (Bison Books, 2007) and *The Resurrection of the Body and the Ruin of the World* (New Issues Poetry Press, 2003). His poems have appeared in *Black Warrior Review, Poetry,* and *Southern Review.*

Mark Halperin. He has published five books of poetry. His most recent is *Falling Through the Music* (University of Notre Dame Press, 2007).

Barbara Hamby. She has published three books of poetry. Her most recent is *Babel* (University of Pittsburgh Press, 2004). She teaches at Florida State University.

David Hernandez. His two books of poetry are *Always Danger* (Southern Illinois University Press, 2006) and *A House Waiting for Music* (Tupelo Press, 2003). His poems have appeared in *AGNI, FIELD, Iowa Review, Missouri Review, Ploughshares, Southern Review,* and *TriQuarterly.*

Margaret Holley. She has published three books of poetry. Her most recent is *Walking Through the Horizon* (University of Arkansas Press, 2006).

Jane Hoogestraat. Her chapbook is *Winnowing Out Our Souls* (FootHills Publishing, 2007). Her poems have appeared in *Crab Orchard Review, DoubleTake, Image, Mars Hill Review, Poetry,* and *Southern Review.* She is a professor of English at Missouri State University.

T. R. Hummer. He has published nine books of poetry. His most recent is *The Infinity Sessions* (Louisiana State University Press, 2005). Hummer is the director of the Creative Writing Program at Arizona State University.

David Ignatow (1914–1997). He wrote over twenty books of poetry. *Living Is What I Wanted: Last Poems* was published posthumously in 1999. Ignatow served as the editor of various journals during his career, including *American Poetry Review, Beloit Poetry Journal,* and *Chelsea.*

Edison Jennings. His poems have appeared in *Boulevard, Kenyon Review, Nebraska Review, Poetry Daily, River Styx,* and *Southern Review.* He teaches at Virginia Intermont College in Bristol, Virginia.

Wayne Johns. His chapbook is *An Invisible Veil Between Us* (Thorngate Road Press, 1997). His poems have appeared in *Green Mountains Review, Image, Lodestar Quarterly, Mid-American Review, Ploughshares,* and *Prairie Schooner.*

William Jolliff. His poems have appeared in *Appalachian Journal, Midwest Quarterly, Northwest Review, Southern Humanities Review,* and *West Branch.*

X. J. Kennedy. He has published eight books of poetry. His most recent is *Peeping Tom's Cabin* (BOA Editions, 2007).

Jesse Lee Kercheval. Her two books of poetry are *Dog Angel* (University of Pittsburgh Press, 2004) and *World as Dictionary* (Carnegie Mellon University Press, 1999). She teaches at the University of Wisconsin, Madison, where she directs the Wisconsin Institute for Creative Writing.

James Kimbrell. His two books of poetry are *My Psychic* (Sarabande Books, 2006) and *The Gatehouse Heaven* (Sarabande Books, 1998). Kimbrell teaches in the creative writing program at Florida State University.

David Kirby. His most recent book of poetry is *The House on Boulevard St.: New and Selected Poems* (Louisiana State University Press, 2007). Kirby is the Robert O. Lawton Distinguished Professor of English at Florida State University.

Kathryn Kirkpatrick. She has published three books of poetry. Her most recent is *Out of the Garden* (Mayapple Press, 2007). She is a professor of English at Appalachian State University in Boone, North Carolina.

Judith Kitchen. Her book of poetry is *Perennials* (Anhinga Press, 1986). An advisory and contributing editor at *Georgia Review,* Kitchen also serves as co-director of the Rainier Writing Workshop low-residency MFA program at Pacific Lutheran University in Washington.

Carolyn Kizer. She has published eight books of poetry. Her most recent is *Cool, Calm & Collected* (Copper Canyon Press, 2000). Kizer founded *Poetry Northwest* in 1959 and remained its editor until 1965.

Ted Kooser. His book of poetry, *Delights & Shadows* (Copper Canyon Press, 2004), won the 2005 Pulitzer Prize. He served as U.S. poet laureate from 2004 to 2006.

Maxine Kumin. Her most recent book of poetry is *Still to Mow* (Norton, 2007). *Up Country: Poems of New England, New and Selected* (Harper & Row, 1972) won the 1973 Pulitzer Prize.

Kurt Leland. His poems have appeared in *Beloit Poetry Journal, Birmingham Poetry Review, Cottonwood,* and *Spoon River Poetry Review.*

Denise Levertov (1923–1997). She published more than twenty volumes of poetry. *This Great Unknowing: Last Poems* was published posthumously by New Directions in 1999.

Lyn Lifshin. Her most recent book of poetry is *Another Woman Who Looks Like Me* (Black Sparrow Press, 2006).

Lou Lipsitz. He has published three books of poetry. His most recent is *Seeking the Hook* (Signal Books, 1998).

Joanne de Longchamps (1923–1983). She wrote seven books of poetry. *Torn by Light,* a collection of her selected poems, was edited by Shaun T. Griffin and published posthumously by the University of Nevada Press in 1993.

B. D. Love. His book of poetry is *Water at the Women's Edge* (Urthona Press, 2002). He teaches writing at California State University, Los Angeles.

Susan Ludvigson. She has published eight books of poetry. Her most recent is *Escaping the House of Certainty* (Louisiana State University Press, 2006).

Peter Makuck. He has published six books of poetry. His most recent is *Off-Season in the Promised Land* (BOA Editions, 2005). Until his retirement in

2006, Makuck was the editor of *Tar River Poetry* and a distinguished professor of American literature at East Carolina University in Greenville, North Carolina.

Adrianne Marcus. She has published three books of poetry and three chapbooks. Her poems have appeared in *ArtLife, Askew, Atlantic Monthly, Epoch, Massachusetts Review, Nation, Near East Review, Nimrod, Paris Review, Poetry Ireland, Poetry New Zealand, Poetry Northwest,* and *Poetry Scotland.*

Debra Marquart. She has published two books of poetry. Her most recent is *From Sweetness* (Pearl Editions, 2002). She is an associate professor of English at Iowa State University.

William Matthews (1942–1997). He published eleven books of poetry. *Search Party: Collected Poems* was published posthumously in 2004 by Houghton Mifflin, edited by his son Sebastian Matthews and friend Stanley Plumley.

Rebecca McClanahan. Her most recent book of poetry is *Deep Light: New and Selected Poems, 1987–2007* (Iris Press, 2007). She teaches in the low-residency MFA program at Queens University in Charlotte, North Carolina.

Michael McFee. His most recent book of poetry is *Shinemaster* (Carnegie Mellon University Press, 2006). He teaches poetry writing at the University of North Carolina, Chapel Hill.

Heather McHugh. She has published seven books of poetry. Her most recent is *Eyeshot* (Wesleyan University Press, 2003). McHugh has served as the writer-in-residence and a professor of English at the University of Washington in Seattle since 1984.

Peter Meinke. He has published fourteen books of poetry. His most recent is *The Contracted World* (University of Pittsburgh Press, 2006). He directed the Writing Workshop at Eckerd College in St. Petersburg, Florida, for many years.

Philip Memmer. His two books of poetry are *Threat of Pleasure* (Word Press, 2008) and *Sweetheart, Baby, Darling* (Word Press, 2004).

Heather Ross Miller. Her most recent book of poetry is *Friends and Assassins* (University of Missouri Press, 1993). She retired from Washington and Lee University as the first Thomas Broadus Distinguished Professor of English.

Jim Wayne Miller (1936–1996). His final book of poetry was *The Brier Poems* (Gnomon Press, 1997).

Vassar Miller (1924–1998). She published ten volumes of poetry. Her final collection, *If I Had Wheels or Love,* was published by Southern Methodist University Press in 1991. She served twice as the poet laureate of Texas.

Judson Mitcham. His most recent book of poetry is *A Little Salvation: Poems Old and New* (University of Georgia Press, 2007). He teaches writing at Mercer University in Macon, Georgia.

Joan Mitchell. Her poetry has appeared in *Puerto del Sol.*

Robert Morgan. His most recent book of poetry is *The Strange Attractor: New and Selected Poems* (Louisiana State University Press, 2004). Morgan has taught at Cornell University since 1971.

Howard Nemerov (1920–1991). He published twelve books of poetry. *The Collected Poems of Howard Nemerov* (University of Chicago Press, 1977) won the Pulitzer Prize and the National Book Award in 1978. He served as the U.S. poet laureate from 1988 to 1990.

Paul Baker Newman (1919–2004). He published four books of poetry and three chapbooks. Newman taught at the University of Puerto Rico in Mayaguez, at Kansas State University, and at Queens College in Charlotte, North Carolina.

Deborah Pierce Nicklas. Her poems have appeared in *Commonweal, Cumberland Poetry Review, Nimrod, Poet Lore,* and *Poetry East.*

Judith Tate O'Brien. Her most recent book of poetry is *Everything That Is Is Connected* (Village Books Press, 2005).

Ed Ochester. His most recent book of poetry is *Unreconstructed: New and Selected Poems* (Autumn House Press, 2007). He edits the Pitt Poetry Series, co-edits *5 AM,* and teaches in the Bennington MFA Writing Seminars.

Sharon Olds. She has published nine books of poetry. Her most recent is *One Secret Thing* (Knopf, 2008). Olds is a professor of English at New York University.

Guy Owen. See the introduction.

Linda Pastan. She has published twelve books of poetry. Her most recent is *Queen of a Rainy Country* (Norton, 2006). She served as the poet laureate of Maryland from 1991 until 1995 and taught at the Bread Loaf Writers' Conference for twenty years.

Veronica Patterson. Her two books of poetry are *Swan, What Shores?* (New York University Press, 2000) and *How to Make a Terrarium* (Cleveland State University Press, 1987). Her poems have appeared in *Beloit Poetry Journal, Cimarron Review, Colorado Review, Indiana Review, Louisville Review, Prairie Schooner,* and *Willow Springs.*

Georgette Perry. Her chapbook is *Bramblecrown* (Cedar Hill Publications, 1999). Her poems have appeared in *Green Fuse* and *Hiram Poetry Review.* She is an assistant editor at *POEM.*

Allan Peterson. His two books of poetry are *All the Lavish in Common* (University of Massachusetts Press, 2006) and *Anonymous Or* (Defined Providence Press, 2002). His poems have appeared in *Bellingham Review, Blackbird, Marlboro Review, Massachusetts Review, Perihelion, Prairie Schooner,* and *Stickman Review.*

Deborah Pope. She has published three books of poetry. Her most recent is *Falling Out of the Sky* (Louisiana State University Press, 1999). Pope is a professor of English at Duke University.

Sam Ragan (1915–1996). His final book of poetry was *Listening for the Wind* (St. Andrews College Press, 1995). Ragan served as the North Carolina poet laureate from 1982 until his death in 1996.

Paul Ramsey (1924–1994). His final book of poetry was *The Keepers* (Irvington Publishers, 1984).

Julia Randall (1924–2005). She published seven books of poetry. Her final book was *The Path to Fairview* (Louisiana State University Press, 1992).

Greg Rappleye. His most recent book of poetry is *Figured Dark* (University of Arkansas Press, 2007).

Ron Rash. He has published three books of poetry. His most recent is *Raising the Dead* (Iris Press, 2002). He teaches at Western Carolina University in Cullowhee, North Carolina.

Jay Rogoff. He has published three books of poetry. His most recent is *The Long Fault* (Louisiana State University Press, 2008). His poems have appeared in *Georgia Review, Kenyon Review, Literary Imagination,* and *Southern Review.*

Lee Rossi. His most recent book of poetry is *Ghost Diary* (Terrapin Press, 2002). His poems have appeared in *Atlanta Review, Beloit Poetry Journal, Chelsea, Heliotrope, Nimrod, Poet Lore, Poetry East, Southeast Review, Tar River Poetry,* and *Wormwood Review.*

Larry Rubin. He has published four books of poetry. His most recent is *Unanswered Calls* (Kendall/Hunt Publishing, 1997). Rubin retired as a professor of English from Georgia Institute of Technology, where he taught from 1955 until 1999.

Gary Sange. He has published two books of poetry. His poems have appeared in *Bellingham Review, Carolina Quarterly, Crazyhorse, Hawaii Review, New Virginia Review, Ohio Review, Seattle Review,* and *Shenandoah.* He is a poetry professor in the MFA program at Virginia Commonwealth University.

James Scruton. His most recent book of poetry is *Galileo's House* (Finishing Line Press, 2004). His poems have appeared in *Hayden's Ferry Review, Poetry, Poetry East,* and *Tar River Poetry.* Scruton is the Humanities Division chair at Bethel College in Tennessee.

James Seay. His most recent book of poetry is *Open Field, Understory: New and Selected Poems* (Louisiana State University Press, 1997). He teaches at the University of North Carolina, Chapel Hill.

Bettie Sellers. She has published four books of poetry. Her most recent is *Wild Ginger* (rpt., Kennesaw State University Press, 2006). Sellers taught at Young Harris College for thirty-one years and served as the poet laureate of Georgia from 1997 until 2001.

Marc J. Sheehan. His book of poetry is *Greatest Hits* (New Issues Poetry Press, 1998). His chapbook is *The Cursive World* (Ridgeway Press, 1991). His poems have appeared in *Apalachee Quarterly, Fine Madness, High Plains Literary Review, Michigan Quarterly Review, Prairie Schooner,* and *Water~Stone.*

Carrie Shipers. Her poems have appeared in *Crab Orchard Review, Meridian, Pleiades, Quarterly West,* and *Spoon River Poetry Review.*

Enid Shomer. She has published four books of poetry. Her most recent is *Stars at Noon: Poems from the Life of Jacqueline Cochran* (University of Arkansas Press, 2001).

Nancy Simpson. Her book of poetry is *Night Student* (State Street Press, 1985). Her chapbook is *Across Water* (State Street Press, 1983). She serves as the resident writer at John C. Campbell Folk School in North Carolina.

David R. Slavitt. He has published seventeen books of poetry. His forthcoming collection is *Sleep Set and Other Poems* (Louisiana State University Press, 2009). Slavitt is an associate fellow of Trumbull College at Yale University and a senior common room associate of Leverett House at Harvard University.

Arthur Smith. He has published three books of poetry. His most recent is *The Late World* (Carnegie Mellon University Press, 2002). Smith is a professor of English at the University of Tennessee, Knoxville.

Charlie Smith. He has published six books of poetry. His most recent is *Women of America* (Norton, 2004). His poems have appeared in *American Poetry Review, Harper's, Nation, New Yorker, Paris Review,* and *Poetry.*

Dave Smith. His most recent book of poetry is *Little Boats, Unsalvaged* (Louisiana State University Press, 2006). Smith is chair of the Writing Seminars and Elliot Coleman Professor of Poetry at Johns Hopkins University.

Ron Smith. His most recent book of poetry is *Moon Road: Poems 1986–2005* (Louisiana State University Press, 2007). He teaches at the University of Richmond.

R. T. Smith. His most recent book of poetry is *Outlaw Style* (University of Arkansas Press, 2007). Smith is the editor of *Shenandoah*.

Katherine Soniat. Her most recent book is *Alluvial* (Bucknell University Press, 2001). *The Swing Girl* is forthcoming (Louisiana State University Press, 2010). Her poems have appeared in *Iowa Review, Kenyon Review, Poetry East, Prairie Schooner,* and *Southern Review*.

William Stafford (1914–1993). His final collection, published posthumously, is *The Way It Is: New and Selected Poems* (Graywolf Press, 1998).

Timothy Steele. His most recent book of poetry is *Toward the Winter Solstice* (Swallow Press/Ohio University Press, 2006).

Lisa Erb Stewart. Her poems have appeared in *Chaminade Literary Review, Honolulu Weekly, Indiana Review, Literary Arts Hawaii, Manoa: A Pacific Journal of International Writing, Sister Stew, Sonora Review,* and *Suisun Valley Review*.

John Stone. His most recent book of poetry is *Music from Apartment 8: New and Selected Poems* (Louisiana State University Press, 2004). Stone is a professor of medicine (cardiology), emeritus, at Emory University School of Medicine and has often taught for the English Department at Emory.

Dabney Stuart. His most recent book of poetry is *Family Preserve* (University of Virginia Press, 2005).

Julie Suk. She has published four books of poetry. Her most recent is *The Dark Takes Aim* (Autumn House Press, 2003).

Eleanor Ross Taylor. She has published five books of poetry. Her most recent is *Late Leisure* (Louisiana State University Press, 1999).

Henry Taylor. His most recent book of poetry is *Crooked Run* (Louisiana State University Press, 2006). Taylor is a professor emeritus of literature at American University in Washington, D.C., where he taught from 1971 until 2003. *The Flying Change* (Louisiana State University Press, 1985) won the 1986 Pulitzer Prize.

Randolph Thomas. His poems have appeared in *Hudson Review, Louisiana Literature, Poetry, Quarterly West, Southwest Review, Texas Review,* and *Witness.* Thomas is the Creative Writing Program coordinator at Louisiana State University.

Juanita Tobin (1915–2007). She published five books of poetry. Her final book was *License My Roving Hands* (Parkway Publishers, 2001).

Eric Trethewey. He has published six books of poetry. His most recent are *Heart's Hornbook* (Larkspur Press, 2004) and *Songs and Lamentations* (Word Press, 2004). He teaches literature and creative writing at Hollins University.

Memye Curtis Tucker. Her book of poetry is *The Watchers* (Ohio University Press, 1998). Her poems have appeared in *Colorado Review, Denver Quarterly, Georgia Review, Oxford American, Shenandoah,* and *Southern Review.* She is a senior editor at *Atlanta Review.*

Nance Van Winckel. Her most recent book of poetry is *No Starling* (University of Washington Press, 2007). Her poems have appeared in *Field, Poetry,* and *Poetry Northwest.* She teaches in the MFA programs at Vermont College and Eastern Washington University.

Ronald Wallace. His most recent book of poetry is *For a Limited Time Only* (University of Pittsburgh Press, 2008). Wallace co-directs the creative writing program at the University of Wisconsin–Madison, and he edits the University of Wisconsin Press poetry series.

Robert Watson. He has published six books of poetry. His most recent is *The Pendulum: New and Selected Poems* (Louisiana State University Press, 1995). Watson is a professor emeritus at the University of North Carolina, Greensboro.

Charles Harper Webb. His most recent books of poetry are *Amplified Dog* (Red Hen Press, 2006) and *Hot Popsicles* (University of Wisconsin Press, 2005). He is director of creative writing at California State University, Long Beach.

Ellen Wehle. Her poems have appeared in *New Republic, Notre Dame Review, Poetry, Slate, Southern Review,* and *Versal.*

Will Wells. His book of poetry is *Conversing with the Light* (Anhinga Press, 1988). Wells teaches English and creative writing at Rhodes State College in Ohio.

Robert West. His two chapbooks are *Out of Hand* (Scienter Press, 2007) and *Best Company* (Blink Chapbooks, 2005). His poems have appeared in *Carolina Quarterly, Cortland Review, Pembroke Magazine,* and *Poetry*. West teaches at Mississippi State University.

Dallas Wiebe. His most recent book of poetry is *On the Cross* (Dreamseeker Books, 2005). He is a professor emeritus of English at the University of Cincinnati.

Miller Williams. He has published fifteen books of poetry. His most recent is *Time and the Tilting Earth* (Louisiana State University Press, 2008).

Edward Wilson. His poems have appeared in *American Poetry Review, Beloit Poetry Journal, Midwest Quarterly,* and *Poetry*.

Charles Wright. He has published eighteen books of poetry. His most recent is *Littlefoot* (Farrar, Straus, and Giroux, 2007). *Black Zodiac* (Farrar, Straus, and Giroux, 1997) won the 1998 Pulitzer Prize. Wright is a professor of English at the University of Virginia in Charlottesville.

Charles David Wright (1931–1978). His two books of poetry are *Clearing Away* (Confluence Press, 1980) and *Early Rising* (University of North Carolina Press, 1968). He taught at the University of North Carolina, Chapel Hill, in the 1960s, and, in the 1970s, at Boise State University in Idaho.

Katherine E. Young. Her chapbook is *Gentling the Bones* (Finishing Line Press, 2007). Her poems have appeared in *Archipelago, Carolina Quarterly, Iowa Review, Poet Lore,* and *Shenandoah.*

Ed Zahniser. He has published six collections of poetry. His most recent is *Mall-hopping with the Great I AM* (Somondoco Press, 2006). Zahniser is the associate poetry editor of *Antietam Review.*

Author Index

Title Index

Appendix

Guy Owen Prize

	JUDGES	WINNERS
1983	The Editors	Coleman Barks
1984	Siv Cedering	William Pitt Root
1985	Peter Wild	David Kirby
1986	Linda Pastan	Ron Smith
1987	Henry Taylor	Joe Bolton
1988	Gerald Stern	Sue Ellen Thompson
1989	David Bottoms	Anya Achtenberg
1990	Betty Adcock	LuAnn Keener
1991	Susan Ludvigson	Robert Boyd
1992	James Tate	Suzanne Cleary
1993	Charles Simic	Debra Marquart
1994	Stephen Dobyns	B. H. Fairchild
1995	Diane Wakoski	Erika Lenz
1996	Mary Oliver	Gwen Ebert
1997	Jane Hirshfield	Ted Genoways
1998	Walt McDonald	Ted Genoways
1999	Dana Gioia	Angie Estes
2000	Li-Young Lee	Rebecca Warren
2001	Ken McLaurin	Juliet Rodeman
2002	Peter Meinke	Debra A. Daniel
2003	Ellen Bryant Voigt	Andrew Grace
2004	David Kirby	Alison Jarvis
2005	Fred Chappell	Enid Shomer
2006	Dave Smith	R. T. Smith
2007	Linda Pastan	Marianna Busching
2008	Jane Hirshfield	George David Clark

JAMES SMITH is associate professor of English at
Armstrong Atlantic State University and associate
editor of *Southern Poetry Review.*

BILLY COLLINS is former two-time U.S. Poet Laureate
and the author of several books of poetry, including
The Apple that Astonished Paris, his first book, published
by the University of Arkansas Press in 1988.